THE
HEDGE BOOK

How to Select, Plant, and Grow a Living Fence

JEFFREY WHITEHEAD

A Garden Way Publishing Book

Storey Communications, Inc.
Schoolhouse Road
Pownal, Vermont 05261

Cover and text design by Carol Jessop
Cover photograph © Derek Fell
Interior color photographs © Derek Fell unless otherwise noted
Illustrations in chapters 7&8 by Brigita Fuhrman; all others by Carol Jessop
Edited by Jill Mason
Indexed by Kathleen D. Bagioni
Color printing in the United States by Excelsior Printing

The name Garden Way Publishing is licensed to Storey Communications, Inc., by Garden Way, Inc.

Printed in the United States by The Book Press
First printing, September 1991

Library of Congress Cataloging-in-Publication Data

Whitehead, Jeffrey, 1956-
          The hedge book : how to select, plant, and grow a living fence /
    Jeffrey Whitehead.
              p.   cm.
          Includes bibliographical references and index.
          ISBN 0-88266-742-4 — ISBN 0-88266-695-9 (pbk.)
          1. Hedges.   I. Title.
    SB437.W47   1991
    635.9'76—dc20   91-55014
                                                                  CIP

To my father,
who planted the hedge, long ago,
at the beginning of this book.

CONTENTS

THE LIVING FENCE

The hedge is a compromise in the best sense of the word. Structurally, it is part of the architecture imposed on the landscape by human needs for shelter and territory. Materially, it is part of the natural world, responsive to the dynamics of seasonal progression. The fruit of this compromise is revealed in the simple, harmonious integration of two different systems.

Because hedges contain both the control of architecture and the complexity of the natural world, they relate to both worlds the way a fence cannot. Even a rigidly pruned hedge is less of a landscape imposition than any fence, simply because it is alive. A well-chosen hedge can do far more than block an awful view. It can muffle noise, keep children in or out, allow privacy outdoors, integrate the structure of a building with the landscape — and produce flowers. It's impossible to watch the seasons change in a stockade fence, just as it's impossible to keep a dog off a property demarcated by nothing more than its carefully manicured appearance.

This dual nature of hedges allows a gradual integration of home and environment, whatever and wherever they may be. In semi-rural areas, the woodlands and meadows can be connected to home or office building with an informal hedge, which defines the space around the building while welcoming the natural world surrounding it. In densely populated suburbs, especially new subdivisions with small trees, the hedge becomes a conduit, allowing nature to enter, with its birds, patterns, and flowers. In

the central city, where tall buildings substitute for trees and burger pods replace leaf litter, a formal hedge echoes the flat walls as it wraps a small courtyard with greenery. Hedges adapt to nearly any landscape because they are so variable: formal or informal, deciduous or evergreen, of varying height and changing colors.

The main reason for hedging is the delineation of territory. The versatility of hedges becomes clear when our wide range of territorial needs is considered: making a simple, friendly distinction between neighbors' yards, separating a quiet patio from a back yard aswarm with children, defining the sprawling front yard of a large property, or putting a border around a garden.

A hedge can screen out changes that occur on adjacent properties, as well as the sometimes objectionable trappings of the occupants, while allowing visual ownership of their trees and tall shrubs. Japanese landscape architects call this principle "borrowed landscape." It is also known as eating the cake you do not own. The hedge allows this expansion of one's visual territory because it is of the same natural fabric as the borrowed trees. It stops what needs stopping, includes what needs including.

Further, the hedge is usually a friendly structure. When properties are close together, a divider made of shrubbery will match, better than a fence, the neighbor's landscape, which also includes grass, shrubs, and trees. Around gardens, play-yards, pools, and patios, hedges subdivide space to create intimacy, provide barriers to children, and frame gardens — essentially, bring the big outdoors down to a personal scale.

On commercial or corporate properties, the hedge can act in similar, though less varied ways. It can enclose a terrace for employees to enjoy their lunch, creating a more casual and relaxing space than may be available in the larger workplace. As

on any property, a relatively small area framed by a hedge can be a place to collect one's thoughts in an outdoor environment.

On a large property, private or corporate, a hedge can carry architectural commands far into the landscape. A broad expanse of space leading up to a building is best defined by a forest edge or a hedge that is proportionate to the building. A tremendous sweep of tall, clipped spruce trees, stoic and green throughout the seasons, can reflect a personal or corporate attitude across a distance. Evergreen hedges tend to reinforce the unchanging lines of brick, concrete, stucco, and painted-wood surfaces.

A quite different effect is achieved when a glass-and-metal building or a natural-wood building with plenty of windows is connected to the surrounding landscape with a deciduous hedge. The home or office building may be just as large as the one in the evergreen example, but the deciduous hedgeplants, responsive to wind and the whims of the seasons, will be reflected in the glass and on the wood. The hedges in both cases can define a large space, but the attitudes projected by the architecture, and by extension, the owner, are nearly opposite: in the former case a static, wall-like hedge is used to separate nature's complexity from the property, whereas in the latter case nature's complexity is welcomed and magnified. In both, however, the visual impact of the structure is enhanced, as it blends into the environment.

Landscapes need a balance of neutral greenery and eye-catching shapes and colors to be pleasing; a non-flowering hedge, let's say Canada hemlock, used as a backdrop to a perennial garden, exemplifies this perfectly. The fact that this hedge also mimics the flat side of the house forty feet away, thereby helping to integrate the house and garden into one harmonious unit, only enhances its usefulness. (Further, if the hemlock hedge is clipped once a year in the spring, the lacy new growth with silvery

undersides will be evident in winter, when the garden is quiet.)

Though nearly every plant at one time or another has been shaped into something resembling a hedge (certain mosses and algae excepted), hedgeplants are primarily selected for small leaves (proportional to common hedge size), twigginess (for density), and the capacity to withstand regular pruning. Obviously, many other aspects of the plant sneak in as well — flowers, twig texture, leaf shape, scent, seasonal color, and fruit are a few of the more noticeable. Even on formal hedges, carefully scheduled pruning can allow flowers and fruit to be dependable features.

The hedge constitutes a friendly intermediate between the rigid, linear architecture of human beings and the complex designs of nature. It acts as a semi-permeable membrane between the personal scale and the larger communities of plants and people, allowing only what we wish to pass through, by design and manipulation. A hedge strikes the right chord between our aesthetic and territorial frameworks because, unlike any other part of the vegetative complex surrounding us, it exists to separate and secure our position. Shrubbery, lawns, even gardens grade subtly or conspiratorily into the larger, unowned Nature Beyond. Though a leaf-carrying member of that world, the hedgeplant serves our purposes without the antagonism of a chain-link fence. And since that world beyond often includes neighbors, the hedge's friendliness is indispensable in maintaining goodwill as well as demarcation of territory.

SECTION 1

CHAPTER 1
HEDGES & LANDSCAPE DESIGN

H edges either *define* or *re*define a space. We start with a space, a place we use for something: Run the dog. Store a boat. Sip gin-and-tonics. Let kids play. If that space is a yard on a newly developed lot, it is raw, and needs to be sectioned into one or several areas with differing purposes. If the space is an established one, perhaps a home in an older neighborhood, the new owners will want to change the way the spaces are used.

When we use a hedge to define a space, we are concerned entirely with what we *want*. For example, the B. Green family has a yard in a new subdivision. (See the sketch on page 3.) They like the greenway space to the north of their house. It is a restored prairie, with a bike trail coursing through it. Kids use the greenway to play and as a shortcut to school and a park. The hedge the Greens develop along the north side of their property defines what they want: It lets the kids and dog-walkers of the greenway know that the Greens' land begins along the hedgeline. But it is not exclusive — the greenway is pretty, and so the hedge is low, 3 or at most 4 feet tall — it lets the Greens have visual ownership of the public land, while still gently excluding the public from their back yard.

Hedges used in this two-way manner create a friendly definition: Here is my property line. Since the hedge is part of the greenery, it promotes a visual peace; it's not an aggressive *keep out!* It simply enforces a partial exclusion: walkers and bikers cannot cross the line, but eyes can.

The west side of the house is a different matter. A jagged slab of condominiums project 6-foot-high decks to within 10 feet of

the Greens' property line. The Greens have nothing against condos in general, but those in their back yard, especially those that are elevated and give their incessantly steak-grilling occupants little else to look at but the Greens' back yard, are another matter entirely. The hedge here, to block this view, will redefine space: from steak-grilling condo deck to greenery.

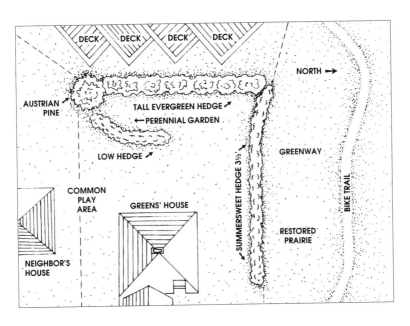

This is a one-way hedge, used to exclude both feet and vision. (The steak-grilling neighbors are happy about this hedge, too. Instead of feeling guilty about their inadvertent voyeurism, they watch the comings and goings of bird life in the greenery.) This hedge (evergreen, of course) provides the perfect backdrop for the Greens' perennial garden. To define a space to protect the garden, they put in another hedge, very low, to steer the kids and their half-blind dog away from the flowers. This third hedge is like the first: it is two-way, including vision but steering little feet away.

This example illustrates the two basic reasons for hedging:

redefining something we don't want to see into something we wish to see, or *defining* an area for a purpose, while still including the best of both sides.

Ideally, you should spend about a year thinking about how your outdoor living spaces are and will be used, before putting up a relatively permanent structure like a hedge. Homeowners too often make reflexive assumptions as to where hedges should go, then arrange their behavior to conform to the limitations the hedgeline makes. The house-and-wall analogy — which says my yard is like a house and needs walls to enclose it — by which many hedges are designed, often gets taken too blindly, without consideration of the fundamental differences between walls and hedges. I think the analogy is valid in the sense that hedges, walls, fences, and shade trees all work to make space more personal. A room, outdoors or in, is protective; it allows us to situate the personal trappings around which we feel comfortable: doghouse, swingset, table and chairs, flowerbed. But the analogy quickly loses validity when pursued much further: the north wall of the house and a hedge along the north property line both block winter wind, but the wall is an integral part of a structure and the hedge is not.

In the next sketch, on page 5, hedge A, hastily put up with little thought to its overall purpose or function, has a hole in it where kids cut through, blocks the best view from the back yard, and needs to be 20 feet taller to function as an effective windbreak, which was its vague purpose. Hedge B illustrates a much better solution: it is planted 15 feet from the house, so it doesn't have to be nearly as tall to block wind effectively; it preserves the view from most windows and allows kids quick access to the next street. Further, it creates a storage area for a well-loved but shabby fishing boat, a woodpile, and the trash cans.

Of course there are many situations in which it is immediately clear where a hedge has to go: The Greens knew before moving in that the view of the condos had to go. But it may have been

unclear that the other two hedges were necessary for some time. Had they moved in and promptly planted the perimeter of the property with a tall hedge, the one along the south side would have been a bad investment. Their kids play with the neighbors' kids

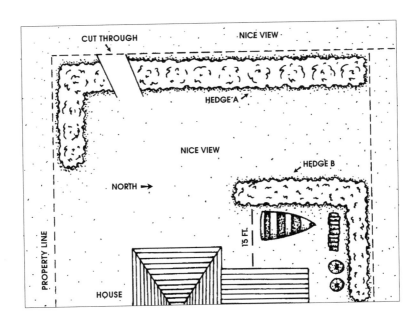

all summer long in the one big space created by their two yards. And it wasn't until a couple of games got out of hand and the perennials got squashed that the need for the low hedge became apparent. Watching the prairie bloom over the seasons convinced them that any hedge along the north side would also have to be low. (The species that was chosen is summersweet, *Clethra alnifolia*. It fits well with the native landscape it faces: it is deciduous, flowers dependably, looks fine with an annual pruning, and tolerates the seasonally wet soil in that part of the yard.)

Whether your ideas for hedge placement arrive slowly, as time, thinking, and money allow, or from obvious, urgent need, chanc-

es for regret diminish greatly after careful planning. Clear purpose, good design, and logical placement of a hedge help to avoid the frustration of trying to adapt to a space unfit for your needs.

Before settling down to the job of selecting a hedgeplant, two more design steps should be taken. First, think of all the possible reasons you can *not* to put a hedge in the spot you have chosen. Then try to refute them. For instance:

Q: Is 6 feet too close to the driveway? What about a snowy winter? Where will the snow go?

A: If we ever get a snowy winter, I'll celebrate by getting a snow thrower that'll pitch the snow over the hedge. I can also be sure to select a hedgeplant that will easily be kept narrow.

Q: Will the neighbors be offended?

A: I don't know. They're hard to figure. I'll let them know what I'm doing before I start digging, though, so they won't be taken aback. Maybe I'll let them know I considered an orange chain-link fence.

Q: Will the hedge block the morning sun in the kitchen?

A: Don't be silly. The hedge'll be only 5 feet tall.

And so on. Second, mark out the hedge with stakes and ropes (preferably set at the anticipated mature dimension). Actually, a garden hose looped into the shape of the proposed hedge, or garbage cans and boxes lined up will do — anything that will help you visualize the general dimensions, bulk, and impact. All I need is a garden hose to give me an idea of what the hedge will do to the landscape, but many people need to see what sort of space it takes up (and imposes). I have often heard homeowners say they

had *no idea* the garden or structure I designed and installed would look the way it did, despite my best efforts to sketch and describe it. Usually it turned out better than they thought it would, but there is no point in taking chances when this last step is so easy.

CHAPTER 2

CHOOSING A HEDGEPLANT

There are three factors that need to be accounted for when choosing a hedgeplant: the ideal, the situation, and the care. Any plant on the resulting list of possibilities will contain the elements needed for a successful hedge.

THE IDEAL

What do you want this hedge to accomplish? Is it to be simply a living wall, whose virtue is being alive yet static? Or do you want a line of not only shiny green, but also silver-brown, yellow, and orange-red by season? Is it only for aesthetic reasons, or do you have a function in mind, as well, such as keeping out the neighbor's dog or blocking an offensive view? See pages 9-10 for a list of purposes for hedging, each with specific features of hedges that will contribute to accomplishing that purpose. Obviously, these features are affected by situation and care and do not stand alone. Since any one hedgeplant will offer several features that contribute to different purposes, it might be best to rank your reasons according to what is most important to you.

THE SITUATION

Soil type and pH, climate zone, exposure to wind, humidity levels, shade conditions, habits of neighbors, pollution, soil compaction, rainfall, and even local animal populations are factors that can affect the success of a hedge and that are, more or less, out of your control. Obviously, these factors affect all landscape plants, but hedges are especially vulnerable for several reasons. First, a few struggling or failed plants in the general landscape are barely

FENCE TO KEEP OUT UNWELCOME CREATURES:

thorniness
stiff, dense branching
thickly branched to base
wide and medium height

FENCE TO KEEP IN WELCOME CREATURES:

stiff, dense branching
thickly branched to base
wide and medium or tall

NEUTRAL WALL OR ARCHITECTURAL EXTENSION:

evergreen
dense, twiggy
slow growth
complex, stiff branching (on deciduous plants)
ice/snow damage-resistant
tolerant of compacted soils
small, even-textured leaves
little or no fruiting or flowering

SHIELD FROM AWFUL SIGHT:

evergreen
dense, vigorous growth
medium or tall
if deciduous: extreme twigginess
if deciduous: leafs out early, holds leaves late

FORMAL FENCE SUBSTITUTE:

fine texture of leaves, twigs
tolerates frequent shearing
slow growth

rigid branch structure
consistently leafy to base

THREE- OR FOUR-SEASON INTEREST:

deciduous
bright autumn color
flowers even if sheared
holds fruits after leaf drop
twig structure/texture interest
glossy or textured leaves
unusual plant for area/neighborhood
leaves change color as they unfold in spring

TOLERANCE OF FREQUENT DAMAGE (SNOW, FOOTBALLS):

deciduous
fast growth
basal growth habits (suckers)

NOISE MUFFLING:

evergreen
pollution-tolerant
dense throughout
wide
thickly branched to base

WINDBREAK:*

evergreen
drought-tolerant
tall, dense growth habits
wide, branched to base

* True windbreaks require a good deal of space to be effective;
hedges work as windbreaks only on a small scale.

noticed; in a hedge they make the whole thing look bad. Second, a hedge is usually the biggest one-time expense in a landscape planting, and less should be left to chance. Third, a hedge may march from a sunny, exposed spot next to a busy street with compacted soil and pollution to the clean air, light shade, and protected conditions of a back yard, therefore being answerable to a much wider range of conditions than the specimen tree at the patio corner.

Listed below are a number of situational factors with comments on how they can affect hedgeplants. (In Section 2 of this book the adaptability of each recommended species to these factors is noted if it is relevant.)

Animals. Rabbits and mice are the usual worry. They gnaw at the bark at ground level in summer and at the snowline in winter. This can damage or kill the plant; however, it is usually limited to young plants. Winter is the only time of year that control measures are worth worrying about. Fencing works, but is time consuming and often ugly. Several commercial preparations are available, such as dried blood, which also works as a fertilizer. (Dried blood is one of the oldest and most effective repellents for rodents and rabbits. It is a by-product of the meat industry. The primary drawback is its short period of effectiveness — a few weeks to a month before a new application is needed. It is sprinkled on the ground, or snow, around the stems.) Some species are especially attractive to rodents; if other landscape plants on your property have suffered damage in the past, it is best to plant unappealing species.

Climate zone. The USDA climate zone map is reprinted on page 12. It roughly delineates zones of average annual minimum temperature, a critical factor in plant hardiness. These lines are not absolute, obviously, but rather strongly advisory. Often, it is the microclimate (the area immediately surrounding a planting) that determines the range of a species' adaptability. For instance,

many species listed as Zone 4 can be grown in protected parts of Zone 3 — actually pockets of Zone 4 found in Zone 3. These pockets might be against evergreens near the top of a hill, away from the cold air downhill. Further, many species vary within themselves as to their hardiness, depending on seed source. A Georgia-bred mountain-laurel may be a Zone 6, while one from the hills of western Massachusetts will be hardy in Zone 4.

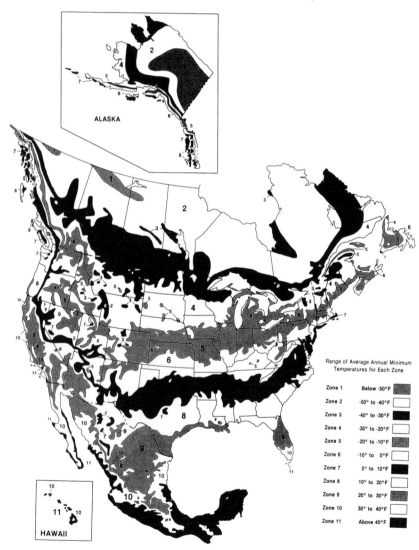

Range of Average Annual Minimum Temperatures for Each Zone

Zone 1	Below -50°F
Zone 2	-50° to -40°F
Zone 3	-40° to -30°F
Zone 4	-30° to -20°F
Zone 5	-20° to -10°F
Zone 6	-10° to 0°F
Zone 7	0° to 10°F
Zone 8	10° to 20°F
Zone 9	20° to 30°F
Zone 10	30° to 40°F
Zone 11	Above 40°F

Humidity. The humid summers of southeast Canada, the upper Great Lakes states, and New England are perfect for such plants as Norway spruce, white pine, and Canada hemlock. These same plants, while cold-adapted elsewhere, require summer humidity to thrive.

Neighbors' habits. A catchall category that can include problems in several areas. Hedges used to block a view of railroad tracks, for instance, may be damaged by herbicide spraying by the railroad company. Chemically hyperactive neighbors, perhaps fanatical about a weed-free lawn, can contribute to injury or death of sensitive hedgeplants. If you know that a hedge may be subjected to herbicide drift, you can select hedgeplants that will tolerate some exposure. Another common problem is the hedge planted too close to the property line — even with pruning, hedges increase in width, and your neighbor has the legal right to hack back a hedge encroaching on his or her property. Profoundly territorial male dogs can cause dead spots on evergreen hedges; I have little to suggest in regard to that problem. Clearly, the list here could go on, but since hedges are beneficial on both sides of the boundary, problems can usually be worked out.

Pollution levels. A susceptible plant next to a very busy street in a small city will suffer more from pollution problems than will the same hedgeplant species on a quiet street in a big city, since the automobile is by far the biggest contributor to pollution. Species listed in Section 2 as pollution-tolerant are the best bets in polluted areas.

Rainfall. Certain species, such as the Canada hemlock, require soil that is evenly moist at all times. If you insist on planting a hedgeplant that requires steady soil moisture in a climate unwilling to provide it, you must make a long-term commitment to providing artificial rain. All else being equal, a plant listed in Section 2 as low-maintenance will be able to survive on natural rainfall.

Shade conditions. Degree of shade is defined in different ways. Half-shade means the area gets full sun for half of each day, as it emerges from behind trees or a building. Full shade is the total, or near-total, lack of direct sun, found on the north side of a building or under a dense canopy of trees. Areas receiving light shade get little full sun but lots of indirect light. This condition is found under tall deciduous trees or below reflective buildings in cities. It is important to consider shade, including future shade from nearby young trees, when planting, since most hedges and hedgeplants do best in a maximum of sun. Maximum use of sunlight is achieved by pruning hedges wider at the base than at the top. This helps prevent loss of lower branches by self-shading.

Soil compaction. Foot traffic, construction equipment, sidewalks, and driveways all contribute to compacted soil, which reduces the amount of oxygen in the soil and disrupts other important soil life-support systems. It takes soil years and years to recover from compaction, hence past compaction is as important to know about as present or future factors contributing to it. Poor drainage is usually indicative of the problem. Some plants are tolerant of compacted soils; many are not.

Soil pH. This is one of the situational factors that can be modified to suit your needs. pH is a relative measure of how acid (sour) or alkaline (sweet) a soil is. Some plants are quite flexible as to the range of pH they will tolerate in the soil; others have more specific requirements. pH is measured on a scale of 1 to 14, with 1 the most acidic, 14 the most alkaline, and 7 neutral. In this book, the term *acid soil* means a soil in the 4.8 to 6.5 range. Most garden soils fall in the upper end of that range. *Alkaline soils* — those developed from limestone — commonly range from 7.0 to 8.5.

If, for instance, you wish to plant mountain-laurel in a soil with a pH of 7.5 (and all other factors favor the growth of mountain-laurel), you will need to decrease the pH about a hundredfold — to a pH of 5.5 or so. To do this, a two-point approach should be

followed. The planting trench should be doubled in width and depth and acidic organic matter worked into the broken soil — peat moss and pine needles are commonly available. Then, finely powdered sulfur should be thoroughly mixed with the soil at the rate recommended on the label, and watered. A waiting period of at least a month is needed before planting.

Conversely, acid soil can be made more alkaline (from a pH of 4.5 to 6.0 for instance) by the addition of lime. Dolomitic limestone is best because it contains magnesium (an essential element) as well as calcium. Usually, lime need be added only every three to five years to maintain the required pH.

Clearly, before soil alterations are made, a soil test is needed. Soil-test kits, in my opinion, are a waste of time and money due to the inexperience of the tester and the inherent inaccuracy of the test materials or equipment. It is best to have the local county Extension Service test a few samples you send them; it is an inexpensive and accurate way to go.

Soil type. I have always found it amusing that many people love to groan on and on about how bad, clayey, acid, rocky, etc., their soil is, as their plants grow lushly about them oblivious to these complaints. Plants mostly grow. Picking a hedgeplant adapted to your existing soil is easier than having to change the soil that's already there, but, like the pH, soil type can be modified to suit your desire for a specific species, all other factors being equal.

Essentially, a soil is either sandy/gravelly, clayey, or in-between. Clay soils are mostly made up of tiny particles that pack tightly together, preventing easy drainage. Sandy/gravelly soils have large particles that allow water to drain fast; they are often dry. It is the soil in-between that is best for most species, though many are perfectly happy in less-than-ideal soils. In-between soils are composed of equal parts clay-sized, middle-sized, and sand-sized particles. *Loam* is the name for this soil type, though it is usually simply called *good.* Clay soils can be improved by

adding organic matter and sand; sandy soils are best improved by adding organic matter (and clay, if available).

It is the organic matter that "completes" a soil of any structure. Organic matter helps make essential chemicals available to roots; it creates conditions needed for important microorganisms and fungi; it fertilizes as it decomposes; and it improves water-holding and water-draining capacity. I should note that soil color is no good indication of fertility; in fact, some black soils are virtually sterile. For advice on modifying special, local soil types such as hardpan, it is best to consult your local county Extension agent.

Wind. Sites subjected to sweeping winds are difficult for many plants. Chronically windy areas, though, often have gentler microclimates, places protected from winds by windbreaks, forest patches, fences, or geographic factors. The worst problem for susceptible plants at windy sites is excessive moisture loss from the leaves. Occasionally, some species ordinarily at risk at a windy site will do fine if there is a steady, all-year moisture supply from the soil. The most damaging winds are the dry, sweeping winter winds, which often occur when soil moisture is locked up by ice. Species adapted to windy, dry places are so noted in Section 2.

THE CARE

Once you know what you want your hedge to be, and the situation in which it will be growing, the last factor that must be addressed is the amount of time and care you are willing to give it.

The degree of formality you want in a hedge is fortunately not closely tied to the amount of work you direct toward it, as there are several hedgeplants I classify as low-maintenance that are also quite formal by nature. A plant designated as low-mainte-nance in Section 2 will require only a few hours of work twice a year or less, once it is established. The work will entail a clipping or shearing once annually or less, weeding young hedges (mature

hedges out-compete most weeds), re-mulching once every few years, picking out wind-blown litter and leaves, fertilizing the hedge grown on nutrient-poor soil, removing the odd broken branch, and knocking off wet snow on young hedges.

These chores will rarely take more than six to eight hours per year for the low-maintenance hedge. Higher-maintenance hedges require more pruning, sometimes up to three times a year, and more careful attention. Some species, such as young white pine, require hand pruning — that is, without electric shears. More skill and planning are also required in pruning some species, which, though tremendously rewarding, have habits of growth not easily convinced to conform into a hedge shape. Fortunately, for nearly all hedgeplants proper care tends to create a self-perpetuating system where twigginess begets more twigginess, which slows growth and creates the density needed to suppress weeds, and strengthens the hedge structure.

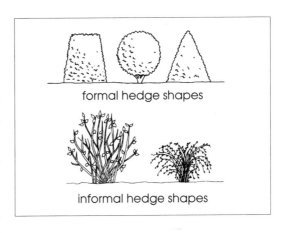

formal hedge shapes

informal hedge shapes

Once the ideal purpose for your hedge is established, as well as the situation and care, a review of the species in Section 2 will leave you with a list of good hedgeplants from which to choose.

CHAPTER 3

BUYING A HEDGE

Buying a hedge is a fairly expensive affair, and the results are something with which you will live for a long time. In fact, a well-selected hedge will probably see more than one owner; it is an investment, one that pays dividends in aesthetics and property value.

Beware of buying plants from a salesperson who is not a professional horticulturist. Since individual hedgeplants are subordinate parts of a whole, they should be selected for uniformity, not the way one would select a specimen tree. Consult both the salesperson's judgment and your own, as well as carefully checking the tags. Taking the plants aside and putting them in a row is a good idea, a time to inspect them for similarity of leaves, twigs, growth habit, and any special features such as flowers. An orange quince in a line of hot pinks looks terrible. More subtle, but equally bad, is mixing different textures and growth habits. The burning bush, *Euonymus alatus*, is often seen mixed with or adjacent to the compact burning bush, *Euonymus alatus* 'Compactus'. At a glance they look similar, yet the compact burning bush is less hardy, has red instead of pink fall color, is finer-textured, has a more upright growth habit, is slower growing, and lacks the corky wings on the twigs. Together they make an awkward hedge.

When choosing evergreen hedgeplants, be sure to buy plants that are branched right down to the ground. Most deciduous plants will be cut back sharply at planting time, so it is important to get plants with strong top growth and large root balls.

Buying closest to the source is the best way to go. That is, a

nursery is preferable to a garden center, which are both vastly preferable to the garden section of a discount store. Quality and accuracy of labelling are best counted on at a nursery, as they are most likely to have professional horticulturists dealing with the growing, labelling, and selling.

Buying close to the source should be taken another way, too: plants grown relatively close to your landscape are better suited for life there due to experience and, often, genetic adaptation. Most plants at discount stores, many at garden centers, and even some at nurseries have been shipped in from a wholesale grower. Sometimes they were grown hundreds of miles away, such as Texas-grown crabapples sold at a Massachusetts garden center. Reputable wholesalers in the South and on the West Coast use genetic sources adapted to the area in which they will be sold, but, all else being equal, the plant grown in a regional nursery is probably the best bet for success on your property.

In areas with hot summers, spring and autumn are the best times to plant, because cooler temperatures and plenty of water minimize transplanting stress. For most plants, it makes no difference if you plant in spring or early autumn. Garden centers and nurseries offering pre-dug plants are anxious to rid themselves of their inventory, because it is expensive and risky to overwinter the stock for spring sales. This is especially true for balled-and-burlapped plants. For common hedgeplants such as Canada hemlock, Ibolium privet, and winged burning bush, this often translates into drastic price reductions in September and October. There are a few species that should only be planted in the spring; these are noted in Section 2.

A few deciduous plants such as the burning bush and the compact cranberrybush viburnum can be spared the severe cutting back that most deciduous plants require. Unless they are container-grown, they should have about a third of their top growth removed at planting, so less-than-perfect plants, provided

they are healthy, are often good buys. Some nurseries offer "hedge-grade" plants, often hemlock or spruce, which were grown too close together and have dead sides due to self-shading. This is exactly what is done on purpose to hedges, so these less expensive plants are sometimes the best choice. Further, many nurseries have quantity discounts that allow you to put in a larger hedge, put plants closer together, or buy better-quality hedgeplants.

Buying better-quality hedgeplants is worth considering, because fast-growing, inexpensive hedgeplants can be very expensive later. Often short-lived, their rapid growth means frequent pruning to keep up a semblance of domesticity. Slower-growing, formal-by-nature hedgeplants will be more expensive at first, but may need only one pruning a year, or less. You'll have the option of doing the annual pruning on a nice day, because the growth rate of these hedges is slow enough that they won't look unkempt if you delay the pruning a month or so. The clippings from moderate or slow-growing plants can often be raked under the hedge as mulch; if not, they'll fill up a barrel or two annually, at most. The fast-growing hedges not only produce a lot of clippings needing disposal, but they spend a certain amount of time each year looking ragged unless pruned on schedule. Places that require an explosively growing Siberian elm hedge are few and far between. In fact, I know of none outside Siberia.

CHAPTER 4

PLANTING A HEDGE

Preparing the soil is the most important job when hedge planting. The other jobs — pruning, setting in, mulching, and watering — follow quickly in soil that has been made as congenial as possible for good growth.

The best way to prepare the soil is to dig a trench, and the easiest way to do that is with a rototiller. A trench makes it easier to visualize the hedge before planting, and gives the entire row a fairly uniform soil situation, a contributing factor to uniform growth rate. The trench should be about twice as wide as a balled-and-burlapped root ball, and about one and a half times as deep. Remember, though, that this is a generalization. In a fertile, well-drained soil with lots of organic matter, a trench barely bigger than the root system will suffice. (Container-grown and bare-root plants must have their roots spread out to determine the extent of the root system. Container-grown plants can be especially misleading, as the

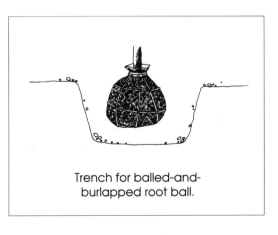

Trench for balled-and-burlapped root ball.

diameter of the pot is *not* the diameter of the root system. The roots are often wound around inside the container and must be teased apart and spread out before planting.)

In soils with serious problems, such as chronic dryness due to

too-sharp drainage, or infertility, or poor drainage due to heavy clay or a subsoil hardpan, a larger trench will allow you to improve the soil in the current as well as the mature root zone.

When installing a hedge along a property line, be sure to plant it in far enough so that at maturity, it will still be entirely on your property. As a rule, hedges will be as wide as tall; a burning bush hedge to be kept 4 feet tall should be planted more than 2 feet in from the boundary. There are some hedges best kept wider than tall, and, fortunately, some species and cultivars that are proportionately much taller than wide.

If grass is growing over the area, cut it out with a shovel, saving it to invert in the bottom of the trench. This, as it decomposes, will provide nutrients for the new roots, as well as improving the water-holding capacity in that important area. If there is no sod, or you want it for patching work elsewhere, spread an inch or two of rotted manure across the trench bottom and mix it well with soil or peat moss.

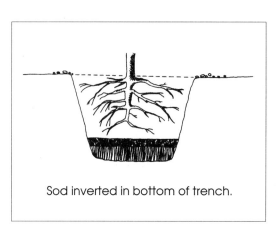

Sod inverted in bottom of trench.

How you prepare the soil you have removed from the trench depends on both the soil quality and the requirements of the particular hedgeplant (see Section 2). Loamy soils with enough organic matter need no improvement. As a general rule, though many plants can grow in poor soils, nearly all species do best in a loamy, well-drained soil. For sandy and dry soils, mix about half the old soil with about half organic matter before you put it back. This organic matter may be of any sort as long as it is not fresh. (Fresh materials include newly cut

grass clippings, vegetable matter, and green leaves, which can produce tremendous amounts of heat as they decompose — enough to kill nearby plant roots. Temperatures in a large pile of fresh organic material can reach 160°F.) Peat moss, peat humus, compost, and old leaves are all fine. Turning under a green manure crop (see Glossary) the season before planting is an excellent way to improve the soil.

Heavy, clayey soils can be made better at draining and have increased oxygen around the roots if you add organic matter, as well as salt-free sand if it is easily available. Plastic drainage pipe, found at hardware stores and farm and builders' supply stores, can be used to improve drainage in difficult situations. The pipe should be placed horizontally at the bottom of the trench and covered with gravel (at least a couple of inches over the top of the pipe). The pipe should have a slight slope and a place to drain away from the hedge. Do not work with clayey soil when it is muddy or wet, for upon drying, compacted clay can turn into a piece of pottery enclosing the roots.

If you are not going to plant the hedgeplants you have purchased right away, they need to be put in a protected spot. Bare-root, container-grown, and dug-up and burlapped plants are in a vulnerable state and need extra care. Crowd container plants close together in a shady or partly shady spot, and water them frequently; in hot weather they may need watering three or more times daily. Bare-root and balled-and-burlapped (B&B) plants should be *healed-in* in a shady spot. *Healing-in* is simply covering up the roots with soil, and keeping the plant well watered. Plants should be crowded together for convenience as well as to conserve water.

PRUNING

Physically, the most difficult work is past, but the hedge-forming sort of pruning now required may be hard psychologically. A

hedge, by definition, is clothed in branches from top to bottom, and should be wider at the base than the top. (This allows sunlight to reach the lowest branches, which are then kept by the plant as productive members.) Evergreens must be well branched when purchased, for it is difficult or impossible to force basal adventitious buds on old wood. Though deciduous plants generally have this ability, with few exceptions their natural form is vase shaped, or wider at the top and open at the bottom. Often on tree hedgeplants there is no branching at all for several feet. Therefore, the fundamental structure of the plant must be altered to create the hedge form.

Deciduous hedgeplants that are not bushy to the base must be cut back sharply. Admittedly, this can be hard to do — taking twenty 6-foot-tall beech trees and lopping them off a foot above the ground seems both sacrilegious and mad. But adventitious buds will sprout below the cut, and a bushy, dense hedge has begun. An outline of the initial pruning hedgeplants will need follows.

At planting time (spring, summer, or fall), cut a third of the top growth out of bare-root and B&B plants, evergreen and deciduous. Plants grown in containers need less pruning, unless the roots are tightly wound around the pot and have to be cut in order to restore a natural, spreading root structure. If this is the case, cut as much from the top of the plant as was cut from the roots. Pruning lessens the stress on transplants, and the closest I can come to a rule is to say nearly all plants should be pruned at planting time. Selectively take out shaded inner branches that will die anyway, as well as any long, goofy, or otherwise misplaced branches. *A season of growth should follow.* Pruning to encourage and maintain good hedge form should begin the year after planting, even if you planted in the autumn.

Shrubs growing in a multi-stemmed suckering fashion should be cut back by half, across the top, to stimulate basal buds. Trees

to be turned into hedgeplants must be cut to within a foot or 6 inches of the ground and fertilized at the same time. However, if suckering shrubs are being planted *after midsummer*, remove no more than a third of the growth *selectively*. That is, follow the guidelines in the preceding paragraph; then, in the spring following planting, proceed to cut back the hedge sharply in the usual manner for suckering shrubs. Midsummer- or fall-planted trees also should be only top-pruned *selectively* at the time of planting. Then, the fol-

Cut back multi-stemmed suckering shrubs by half.

lowing spring, commence with the radical cutting to about a foot above the soil line. (This way the hedge will get its root system established and be ready for a burst of growth in the spring.)

Some cultivars will need no shaping, because they have been asexually propagated (cloned) from a plant that has a desirable hedge form. This includes fastigiate (narrow, strongly upright) and columnar cultivars, such as *Juniperus chinensis* 'Columnaris Glauca'. These cultivars are test-tube shaped and do not have leafy branches at the base. There is no way to force them to become leafy at the ground level, so there is no point in cutting them back sharply. Facer plants must be grown in front of them if a complete visual barrier is necessary.

A few hedgeplants are propagated by budding or grafting above the ground — that is, the desired top is grafted onto a root and trunk stump of another species. Cutting below the graft union could produce an unhappy surprise: French lilac cultivars are often grafted onto the roots of green ash!

PLANTING

Planting is easy. The best planting days are cloudy and cool, with no hot weather in sight. Though summer transplanting is feasible, it requires more work: providing shade, watering more, and correctly timing the pruning.

Bare-root hedgeplants should have their roots soaking in a barrel of water for an hour or so before being planted *one at a time.* Roots should be arranged in a natural, spreading fashion; well-mixed backfill should be sifted or tossed in and about the roots. Periodically, tamp the soil with your hands throughout the root zone to make sure there is full root-soil contact. Large air pockets around dormant bare-root plants can delay or inhibit growth.

Container-grown plants must be pulled from their pots and inspected for root-matting. Often the roots, looking for new territory but finding only plastic, will wind around and around. This, and any other tangled root problems, must be fixed before planting. Tease the outer roots apart, breaking as few as possible, into an outwardly spreading form. This is important, as it is not uncommon to find dead plants in newer landscapes easily uprooted, even after a few years, because their roots failed to escape that strangling pattern of growth.

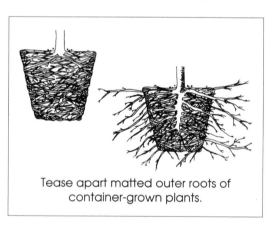

Tease apart matted outer roots of container-grown plants.

Balled-and-burlapped plants should be placed in the trench, burlap and all. Cut away the burlap to expose the top of the root ball. Of course, plastic wraps woven like burlap, should be removed. Never force a root ball into a too-small hole.

During the whole planting operation, the roots cannot be allowed to dry out. The plants in all but chronically wet soils should be set a little lower than the surrounding grade. This will maximize the amount of water that reaches the roots. Soil should be shoveled around the root balls in two stages. After about half is put in, push it down, checking to be sure the backfill additives like peat moss are mixed in well. Water the backfill to help it settle and to keep the plants moist. The final, ritualistic foot-tamping should be just that, not stomping.

Water the hedge immediately after planting. It is important to water heavily, though not often. An hour or two of soaking allows water to penetrate well into the soil, encouraging the roots to grow deep and helping the plant to be more self-sufficient. In spring or fall, new hedges should be watered once a week, or less if it rains heavily. After a month or so of this, gradually taper off. A well-chosen hedge should not need watering after it is established. Young hedges should be watered thoroughly before the ground freezes if the autumn has been a dry one. This is because water requirements do not cease in the winter; they just slow down. As long as the entire root zone is not frozen solid, roots will continue to draw up some water. Canvas soaker hoses are the ideal means to water a hedge; they deliver water at a rate that allows it to penetrate into the deep root zone, with no wasteful runoff or evaporation.

Mulching is one of the best deals in horticulture. A good mulch holds in moisture, suppresses weed growth, allows air through, and keeps the soil temperature steady. Further, most organic mulches will contribute nutrients to the soil as they decay. The best landscape mulches are relatively inexpensive, easy to spread and durable, and won't blow or wash away.

Right after planting is the time to mulch. One to two inches is best in most cases, the minimum required to suppress most weed growth. On dry soils more might be added to help retain moisture,

while on overly moist soils a half inch might be the most you should use. A list of some of the best mulches for hedges follows:

Shredded bark. This is usually the best mulch around. Avoid the chunky or nugget-type of bark; the small sizes can wash away, and the large ones won't work unless quite thick.

Durable leaves. This group includes pine needles, oak leaves, and other types that do not rot easily. Excellent for contributing to and maintaining soil acidity.

Black plastic. This is especially useful for areas of high water loss. To protect it from tearing, as well as for aesthetic reasons, cover it with a thin layer of a heavy, better-looking mulch, such as shredded bark.

Landscape fabrics. These are expensive and well worth it. Various materials are sold by this name, and there are many brands, but generally they are woven or spun-bonded and allow water in but keep weeds out. Because they are not visually appealing, they also should be covered with a *thin* layer of durable organic mulch, like shredded bark.

Peat moss. Peat moss is not recommended for most situations; however, its fine texture and pleasing color may warrant its use in intimate areas, such as around a patio, where coarser mulches won't work aesthetically. It is particularly handsome next to stucco or brick. Otherwise, its drawbacks exclude use as a general mulch: heavy rains can wash it out; when dried it will blow away; and it is hard to re-wet. It also allows surface-sprouting weeds a place to grow.

There are many, many other mulches around. Some are fine; others are more trouble than they are worth. If a mulch is heavy enough not to blow or wash away, is easy to apply and inexpensive, it is worth a try. A few I do not recommend are grass clippings (they mat, and build up heat as they rot), hay of any sort (requires

an absurdly thick layer, harbors rodents, and can introduce weeds), and sawdust (depletes the soil nitrogen).

The newly planted hedge needs only water. Do not fertilize full-strength the year of planting; if you are going to fertilize regularly, begin full-strength fertilization the next year.

CHAPTER 5

PRUNING, SHAPING & FERTILIZING

The single most important thing you can do to create a full, long-lived hedge is shape it correctly. *Correctly* means that it is pruned wider at the base than at the top. This allows a maximum amount of sunlight to reach the lowest branches. Not only does a hedge look good clothed to the ground in leaves, but only a full hedge can do the things hedges are planted to do: insure privacy, act as a fence, shade out the weeds beneath, and so on. Unfortunately, there are vast numbers of bad hedges around, and most result from improper shaping. Often they are next to sidewalks, planted too close, and kept narrower at the base than the top to allow traffic past. These hedges have dead patches in the bottom half due to self-shading, and they look drunk, top heavy. Evergreen hedges pruned in this fashion have often lost the bottom two or three feet of greenery, and the trunks look like legs, as if the hedge is walking away in disgust to some forest where it can grow up with dignity.

Occasionally a vigorous hedge is situated so that one side faces south and must be pruned vertically. As long as the back side is angled wide at the base, this presents no problem. Very low hedges, less than 2½ feet high and situated in full sun, can also be successfully kept with vertical sides for years. Also, hedges that are regularly renewed by cutting back to near ground level can be pruned this way.

The shape of the top is variable, depending on aesthetic and practical factors. Usually in areas where heavy snows are common, round or pointed tops are best, for they will shed the snow easily. A thick layer of snow will squash a flat-topped,

pliable-branched hedge. Sometimes, however, for architectural purposes a flat-topped hedge is needed; there are many rigidly branched hedgeplants available to reduce winter maintenance.

PRUNING

Hedges are pruned to increase density and restrict dimensional growth. This is done by cutting back terminal growth (see Glossary) to force lateral branching. *Hand-pruning* is used here and in Section 2 to mean the selective removal of branches with hand tools; *shearing* is the non-selective removal of branches with electric shears or hedge clippers. Most hedgeplants respond well to shearing, but some do not.

Plants that can be sheared tend to have relatively slender branches and small leaves; this is convenient if they are fast-growing, for shearing greatly reduces time spent on pruning.

The hedgeplants that need hand-pruning fall into a few categories. Some, like the wayfaringtree viburnum and the mountain-laurel, have thick, leathery leaves and woody branches that are damaged by elec-tric shears. The viburnum forms its flower buds for the following year in the last half of summer. Hand-pruning after that time al-lows you to keep a maxi-mum number of future flowers, as the flower buds are easily distinguished from the vegetative buds. Pine hedges, whose growth for each year emerges in

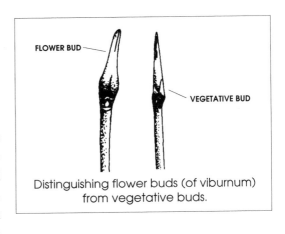

Distinguishing flower buds (of viburnum) from vegetative buds.

May as a *candle*, will need hand-pruning, at least at first. When the candles are about finger length, break the top half off with

your fingers or a very sharp clippers. When the hedge becomes dense and even enough so that most of the candles appear in a plane, shearing is possible, with sharp tools, removing only the top half of the candles.

For most hedgeplants, a single, early-July pruning is all that is needed. Most of the growing for the year is over, and any growth that does come later will tend to be uniform and will have plenty of time to harden-off before fall. Some special cases follow, when pruning at other times is possible or necessary:

Flowering hedges. Hedges that produce multiple branches from the ground, instead of single trunks, need *renewal-pruning* as well as the annual shearing. Examples are border forsythia and gray dogwood. The annual shearing for hedges with showy flowers and no fruiting interest should be done right after flowering. If the flowers will later turn into a red-berry show in winter, as with the compact cranberrybush viburnum, the pruning should be done after the berries drop or are taken by birds, in late winter or early spring.

Renewal-pruning keeps the hedge vigorous over time: it may entail annual removal of the oldest branches at ground level, or periodic cutting back of the entire hedge to about 6 inches from the ground. See Section 2 for the pruning requirements of individual hedgeplants.

Evergreens. Pruning evergreens takes more restraint than pruning deciduous stock. A rule effective for most evergreens is never to cut back to leafless wood, for these plants generally will not produce adventitious buds on old wood. *Taxus* species, the yews; *Ilex* species, the hollies; *Kalmia,* the mountain-laurel; and a few others are more responsive than most to renewing, but even with these, it is best to cut back slowly, always to leafy wood, over a few years.

Although nearly all evergreen hedges can be sheared, hand-pruning usually creates a more interesting, better-textured hedge.

Except pines and spruce, which have their candles clipped in spring, evergreen hedgeplants are best pruned once in late July or August, for they will not put out new growth after that.

Young hedges. After the initial sharp pruning at planting time, let the hedge grow unmolested through the entire first growing season. Between the end of the season and before the following year's growth begins (in fall, winter, or early spring), cut off half of the first-year growth. Especially be sure to remove any central leaders (see Glossary) of hedgeplants née trees, such as beech. Beginning in midsummer of the second growing season, cut off half of each year's new growth. Once the hedge approaches mature size, cutting off all but a centimeter or so of each year's growth is common. Spruce and pine hedges at this stage may have up to two-thirds of the candle removed. At this point, when the hedge is at its useful size, it is obvious why careful planning is needed before planting. A formal hedge of fast-growing stock may now need pruning several times a year, while one of slow-growers may stay quite formal with an every-other-year pruning.

FERTILIZING

Most hedges will not need much fertilizing, since encouraging growth just means more growth that has to be cut off. Slow growth is a desirable feature of a mature hedge. There are, however, situations in which fertilizing is practical or necessary.

Young hedges, beginning the year after planting, can be fertilized to speed the arrival of the mature height. A good way to do this is to topdress the soil each spring or fall with a half inch of rotted cow manure. Another method is to use a general chemical fertilizer, at about 5 pounds per 100 feet of hedge.

Fertilizer is also useful for hedges grown on poor soils, or when an acid-requiring plant is being grown on soil that is alkaline or neutral. In the latter case, fertilizers are available that contribute to soil acidity. With the former, it should be pointed out that there

are several hedgeplants well adapted to grow beautifully on poor, dry, or sterile soils (see Section 2). If you wish to grow a hedge of plants needing loamy, fertile soil in a place with poor soil, not only must the soil in the root zone be greatly modified but also a commitment must be made to a regular fertilizing program.

Still another time to fertilize is after cutting back an old, overgrown deciduous hedge. A healthy layer of cow manure or a general fertilizer will encourage a strong burst of new growth.

CHAPTER 6

PREVENTION & CONTROL

I t is often assumed that plant problems caused by pests, diseases, and environmental factors are best corrected by attacking the problem as soon as the symptoms are made manifest. Not true. *The most effective control measure is prevention.* Haven't we heard this before? Yes, yes, and it's still true.

Planting stock that is disease resistant, sited correctly, and grown in a climate (or microclimate) in which natural plant defenses are optimized prevents most problems from getting started. Carefully following the procedure described in Chapter 2 for choosing a hedgeplant will take you to the point where an insect infestation, disease, or environmentally caused problem is the exception. If you encounter a problem, it can then be handled with the safe assumption that once it is fixed the hedge will thrive.

Most available information on problem control for landscape plants is applicable to hedges as well. However, hedging involves two unnatural situations that can *potentially* increase pest or disease problems:

1. A hedge is a monoculture. Many plants of a single species (or cultivar) grown together are often at a higher risk than just a few of the same species, or cultivar, scattered in a mixed planting. It's easy to see why. When the scale insect, for example, finds a mugho pine and sets up shop, the scale may not spread to the two other mugho pines some distance away in the back yard, with lots of species unacceptable to scale in between. But an infestation on one hedgeplant can quickly spread to the twenty others, all adjacent. This leads to the second, related situation.

2. Hedgeplants are grown under crowded conditions. Crowding slows growth and forces adjacent plants to compete for limited resources. Crowding does good things, too. It creates conditions that are often unfavorable to weed growth, and it evens the growth rate of individual plants. For example, consider an old field strewn with white pine seedlings growing 1½ feet apart. Left alone, one pine in a hundred might survive. But in a hedge, each pine 18 inches from the next is expected to live as a subordinate part of the whole, sharing crowded conditions equally. This may mean that this hedge needs regular, evenly applied fertilizer or complete mouse control to ensure that each plant has the same chance to thrive. One mouse-killed pine, or overly robust pine due to unequal fertilizing, will damage the whole hedge.

Because hedges, along with a few other shade trees and specimen plants, are the most prominent features in a landscape, keeping them healthy is particularly important. Happily, because of their prominence, problems appearing now and then can be quickly noticed. The few blight-blackened shoots on a quince hedge during a prolonged wet spell are obvious and can be removed fast, preventing infection of the whole. Also, the compact, contained form of hedges lends itself easily to control measures, whether it means spraying *Bt* on a pine hedge during a sawfly outbreak, hosing down a Clavey's dwarf honeysuckle to knock back a mite population, or sprinkling a carton of ladybugs on a firethorn hedge to eat the aphids.

I should emphasize that even a well-chosen hedge, properly sited and cared for, will have a few problems over the course of its life. But it is the owner who ultimately defines a problem. Mr. C. may not care when his Chinese lilac hedge gets covered with powdery mildew every August. It really doesn't harm the hedge; the leaf color is still uniform, and perhaps the silvery cast pleases him. For him, powdery mildew is not a problem. Ms. M., on the other hand, gets disgusted each time she sees her Chinese lilac

hedge succumb to powdery mildew. She sees fungus, not leaves, and spraying it with a fungicide at the proper time may be the right course for her.

Minor insect outbreaks occur constantly in nature, but they are usually suppressed by natural controls before they become apparent. If your tolerance level is set above this point, you can save energy and time for the rare outbreak that really requires fixing. Certainly the best approach to keeping a healthy hedge, or landscape, is to understand what problems are likely to come up from time to time. By knowing what causes them, you can take preventative measures, or at least be ready to treat the problem before it causes serious damage. A reasonable way to map strategy might look like this:

Education. Know the hedgeplant's weaknesses and the conditions that trigger them. Example: dwarf Japanese yew. During severe, snowy winters, mice may girdle branches.

Situation. Early, heavy snows cover hedge. Cold keeps snow in place.

Option A: Do nothing. Risk losing some plants or prominent branches to mice. Would have to replace, or wait a few years for hedge to rejuvenate.

Option B: Wait and see; then treat. Lots of work clearing away snow to examine branches for damage. Easy to miss damage.

Option C: Keep hedge zone prophylactically treated by spreading mouse repellent about hedge interior as needed during winter.

When choosing a hedgeplant, it is useful to know what problems might come up. That is the purpose behind the following section. Please remember, after seeing problem after problem lined up behind the hedgeplant of your dreams, that you'll get to know few or none of these if the hedge is well sited. This book covers hedging for a large area, from the border of Zones 4 and 5 northward, so I have tried to be inclusive of pests

and diseases without being compulsive or alarmist. For example, various ills effectively eliminate the alpine currant from consideration over most of New England, but they don't affect this plant much at all in the upper Midwest, where it thrives.

A listing such as that which follows should only be considered background information. Local experts such as Extension agents, nursery people, good gardeners, educated landscapers, and the like will give the most useful advice. *Local* and *experienced* are the key words here: these people can deliver the most useful advice on hedging problems in your area.

ABELIA X GRANDIFLORA (GLOSSY ABELIA)

No serious problems. Winter dieback at the northern edge of its range is the only real physiological problem. This rarely kills the plant, but extensive pruning and re-shaping may be necessary.

ACANTHOPANAX SIEBOLDIANUS (FIVELEAF ARALIA)

No serious problems. Some plant bugs may make brown, circular, punched-in spots on the outer leaves. I've never seen this problem, however, and can't imagine it being worth treating.

ACER GINNALA (AMUR MAPLE)

No serious problems. Scorch (necrotic, or dead areas on the leaves) is a physiological problem caused by limited water supply. Hedges under water stress may show scorch. Windburn (necrotic, frayed edges on outermost leaves) is also due to lack of water. Keep an eye on new hedges and hedges in difficult areas (such as between two concrete strips). During prolonged hot, dry spells, especially if it is windy, provide water or temporary shade.

BERBERIS X CHENAULTII (CHENAULT BARBERRY), B. JULIANAE (WINTERGREEN BARBERRY), B. VERRUCULOSA (WARTY BARBERRY)

No serious problems. Brown leaves at the end of winter are

probably due to sun or wind-caused water stress (winterkill). This is a problem at the northern edge of their range, especially if plants are exposed to sweeping winter winds or afternoon sun. If you insist on planting one of these in an area where they are marginally hardy, proper siting is critical. Also, a thick mulch, a good soaking before the ground freezes, and an anti-desiccant spray are useful.

OTHER *BERBERIS* SPECIES AND HYBRIDS

Barberries are generally free of pests and diseases, though I've occasionally seen rust fungus, mosaic-type virus evidence (mottled leaves), scale, and webworm.

BUXUS SPP. (BOXWOOD)

Leaf spot, mealybugs, scale, webworm, mites, leafminer, and canker are sometimes guilty of attacking boxwood. For physiological problems, see *Berberis x chenaultii.*

CARPINUS BETULUS (EUROPEAN HORNBEAM)

No serious problems.

CHAENOMELES SPECIOSA (FLOWERING QUINCE)

Mostly trouble free. A leaf-spot fungus can cause late summer defoliation. It is not fatal and is prompted, apparently, by prolonged rainy periods. Fire blight and rust fungi are occasional problems. The former causes mushy, wet, blackened new growth; the latter produces fuzzy, rust-colored patches on tender leaves, twigs, and fruit, and may be destructive. Its alternate host is the eastern redcedar, *Juniperus virginiana*, which suffers little.

CHAMAECYPARIS OBTUSA (HINOKI FALSE CYPRESS), *C. PISIFERA* (SAWARA FALSE CYPRESS)

Generally free of problems. On *C. p.* 'Boulevard' I often see a dead

tuft of foliage or two. I don't know why it occurs. Perhaps this cultivar has no more dead branchlets than any other, but because of its unusual blue-furry appearance, the dead ones stand out.

CLETHRA ALNIFOLIA (SUMMERSWEET, SWEET-PEPPER BUSH)

Trouble free unless sited in a chronically hot, dry spot, where spider mites are apt to be a problem.

CORNUS MAS (CORNELIAN-CHERRY DOGWOOD), *C. RACEMOSA* (GRAY DOGWOOD)

No serious problems. Sometimes powdery mildew will make an appearance during a long wet spell on a plant grown in the shade.

C. SERICEA (RED-OSIER DOGWOOD)

Twig blight and canker can be quite serious. Occasionally scale and bagworms will present problems.

COTONEASTER LUCIDUS (HEDGE COTONEASTER)

Mites, blister mites especially, webworm, scale, leaf borer, lace bug, fire blight, canker, and leaf spot can be problems. In my experience, webworm (it skeletonizes the leaves), scale, and blister mites are the most destructive. In most areas, none is serious enough to avoid this species.

CRATAEGUS CRUS-GALLI (COCKSPUR HAWTHORN), *C. PHAENOPYRUM* (WASHINGTON HAWTHORN)

A number of problems affect this genus, and its members should be planted only where their cultural requirements are met. Though leaf-attacking fungi are prevalent on hawthorns in general, these two glossy-leaved species are not nearly as susceptible. Tent caterpillars, mites, aphids, borers, scab, and fire blight are problems at times.

ELEAGNUS ANGUSTIFOLIA (RUSSIAN-OLIVE, OLEASTER)

Healthy, well-kept, and fertilized hedges are prone to few problems. At times, blight, rust, crown gall, aphids, or scale may show up on a stressed hedge.

EUONYMUS ALATUS (WINGED BURNING BUSH), *E. A.* 'COMPACTUS' (COMPACT BURNING BUSH)

No serious problems.

E. FORTUNEI 'VEGETUS', 'SARCOXIE' (WINTERCREEPER)

Scale insect can be serious and can ruin a hedge in a season or two. In some areas planting these cultivars may be asking for trouble. Check with local gardeners and nursery people before considering these cultivars. Scale can be controlled by dormant oil spraying (see Glossary). Crown gall and thrips may occasionally be serious enough to warrant attention, too.

FAGUS SYLVATICA (EUROPEAN BEECH)

Properly sited and managed hedges are usually free of problems. Some that may occur are powdery mildew, leaf spot, canker, and beech-bark disease, the latter caused by a scale insect allowing a fungus to enter. Aphids and borers also are occasional problems.

FORSYTHIA X INTERMEDIA (BORDER FORSYTHIA HYBRIDS)

Generally pest and disease free. Sometimes mites, plant bugs, Japanese weevil, leaf spot, or crown gall are a problem, as can be a dieback caused by a fungus.

Physiological problems include an absence of flowers, especially above the snowline. This is due to winterkill of flower buds, which are not as hardy as the vegetative buds. Since the flowers are the only reason to plant this hedge, if this problem occurs more than once, tear out the hedge and put in a hardier cultivar.

ILEX CRENATA 'CONVEXA' (JAPANESE HOLLY)

No serious pests or diseases. See under *Berberis x chenaultii* for a discussion of winterkill, which can affect this species under similar conditions.

I. GLABRA 'COMPACTA' (COMPACT INKBERRY HOLLY)

Trouble free.

I. OPACA (AMERICAN HOLLY)

This species is plagued with problems and should be grown only in areas where it is known to thrive. If it did not make such a wonderful hedge and have such seasonally useful clippings, it would be hard to justify including it in this book. Leaf miner, scale, bud moth, whitefly, mites, Japanese beetle, berry midge, powdery mildew, tar spot, dieback fungus, canker, and a blight (bacterial) are variously problematic.

A physiological problem is browning of leaves during winter; see the discussion under *Berberis x chenaultii.*

I. VERTICILLATA (WINTERBERRY, BLACK-ALDER)

A few fungus types occasionally attack: powdery mildew, tar spot, leaf spot.

JUNIPERUS CHINENSIS (CHINESE JUNIPER)

Several problems can bother Chinese junipers: bagworm and twig blight are the most serious; others include bark beetle, mites, aphids, scale, cedar-apple rust, and wilt disease.

J. VIRGINIANA (EASTERN RED-CEDAR)

Cedar-apple rust and bagworms are the only noteworthy problems.

KALMIA LATIFOLIA (MOUNTAIN-LAUREL)

Leaf spot, leaf blight, scale, lace bug, azalea stem borer, rhododendron stem borer, whitefly, and black vine weevil will sometimes bother this species.

See under *Berberis x chenaultii* for physiological problems.

KOLKWITZIA AMABILIS (BEAUTYBUSH)

No serious problems.

LARIX DECIDUA (EUROPEAN LARCH), *L. LARICINA* (AMERICAN LARCH, TAMARACK)

The larch case-bearer can be very serious. In mid-spring it eats its way into the needles, causing them to brown. Also aphid, larch sawfly, gypsy moth, Japanese beetle, tussock moth, canker, and needle rust can appear.

LIGUSTRUM AMURENSE (AMUR PRIVET), *LIGUSTRUM X IBOLIUM* (IBOLIUM PRIVET)

Generally free of problems. On plantings under stress, twig blight, leaf spot, privet aphid (rolls up leaf), scale, thrips, mites, Japanese weevil, and mealybugs may become problematic.

LONICERA X XYLOSTEUM 'CLAVEYI' (CLAVEY'S DWARF HONEYSUCKLE)

Mostly free of problems. In hot, dry weather spider mites can be a nuisance.

PHYSOCARPUS (NINEBARK)

No serious problems.

PICEA ABIES (NORWAY SPRUCE)

Healthy, well-kept plantings are pretty tough. Otherwise, a host

of ills are out there and may present problems: canker, rusts, bagworm, spruce gall aphid, cooley spruce gall aphid, spruce budworm, mites, scale, needle miner, sawflies, needle cast, and pine needle scale.

PINUS SPP. (PINES)

Scale is a very serious problem on *Pinus mugo* and prevents using this species in many areas. Sawflies can also be a bad problem. Borers and rust are rarely serious.

On white pine, blister rust, a bark disease, can be serious. White pine blight, a disease of unknown etiology, can brown current season's growth. Sawflies, shoot borer, pine needle scale, tube moth, aphids, and canker are sometimes troublesome. White pine weevil is a serious problem on specimen pines, but actually helps hedges because it kills the terminal shoot and makes the plant bushier.

P. resinosa is sometimes affected by stunt, probably a physiological problem due to poor drainage.

PRINSEPIA (PRINSEPIA)

Trouble free.

PYRACANTHA COCCINEA (FIRETHORN)

Fire blight, scab (turns fruit soot-colored), twig blight, aphids, lace bug, and scale can all be problems, though I'd rate only the first one as serious.

RHUS AROMATICA (FRAGRANT SUMAC)

No serious problems. Rarely, rust, leaf spot, mites, aphids, or scale will crop up.

RIBES ALPINUM (ALPINE CURRANT)

Mites, scale, currant aphid, leaf spot, cane blight, and anthrac-

nose are occasional problems. Rust is serious, and to avoid the problem only the male cultivars, such as 'Green Mound', should be planted.

SYRINGA VILLOSA (LATE LILAC), *S. X CHINENSIS* (CHINESE LILAC)

Powdery mildew will often turn these species grayish by late summer. Leaf spot, bacterial blight, lilac borer, scale, and leaf miner may also present occasional problems.

TAXUS SPP. (YEWS)

Generally, trouble-free plants. Sometimes Taxus mealybug, scale, black vine weevil, needle blight, twig blight, or nematodes will present problems.

See *Berberis x chenaultii* for physiological problems.

THUJA OCCIDENTALIS (ARBORVITAE)

Very few problems affect this genus. Rarely, leaf blight, mealybug, leaf miner, scale, bagworm, or mites will be a problem.

A physiological problem involving leaf browning and subsequent drop is apparently due to rapid temperature changes in winter.

TSUGA CANADENSIS (CANADA HEMLOCK)

When sited correctly, there are few problems. Sometimes looper, scale, hemlock borer, mites, canker, needle rust, or blister rust will crop up.

Physiological problems include sunscorch when temperatures rise near 100°F., as well as browning due to wind or drought injury.

VIBURNUM SPP. (VIBURNUMS)

There are no serious problems in this genus, except with *V. lentago*, which is susceptible to powdery mildew.

SECTION 2

CHAPTER 7

RECOMMENDED HEDGEPLANTS

I have compiled the Recommended Hedgeplants chapter to include the best hardy species and cultivars for hedging in nearly all landscape conditions — seaside, urban, windy/exposed, shade, etc. All chosen hedgeplants have a few excellent features; some have many. Those plants that make fine hedges but either are of borderline hardiness (Zone 5) or have a narrow useful range are collected in Chapter 8. Because I have chosen the best plants for hedging across many categories, Chapter 9 contains cross-listings assembled by feature — hedgeplants for tight spots, bird-attracting, winter color, flowering time, and so on.

The recommended hedgeplants are listed by the Latin binomial, as well as the most familiar common name(s). Short sections cover description, cultural requirements, manipulation (planting, pruning, and maintenance), special characteristics, liabilities, and, when necessary, buying issues.

ACANTHOPANAX SIEBOLDIANUS (FIVELEAF ARALIA)

Description. The fiveleaf aralia is like a fine-textured version of the devil's-walkingstick, every bit as prickly but much more useful. Leaves are palmately compound and dark green, giving the informally pruned hedge a vaguely tropical look. Profuse, slim, thorny branches grow quite upright; this hedge is an excellent barrier. The interesting texture of the foliage makes it a good background hedge for a perennial garden.

Cultural requirements. Zone 4. Grows thick and bushy in full sun; will also grow in mostly shade but will not be as full. Soil may

be acidic or neutral, almost wet to quite dry. An urban-tolerant plant, it will grow in compacted soils and polluted air. Naturally, it also responds well to better conditions.

Manipulation. A fast grower, the fiveleaf aralia hedge may require three shearings a season to maintain a formal appearance. It makes a barrier 3 to 8 feet high, about two-thirds as wide as tall. If room permits, this is a good plant for an informal hedge; an annual clipping will promote useful density as well as show off the foliage. Plant in spring or fall, 2 or 3 feet apart. Fertilize annually in very poor soils.

Fiveleaf aralia

Special characteristics. Adaptability, durability, and pest-free qualities are features of a good hedge. Dense thorniness and size combine to make an effective barrier. Excellent urban hedgeplant, as well as a good hedge for textural effects in less trying situations. Repellent to children, dogs, and others of that ilk.

Liabilities. Snow and odd flying objects can break branches easily, but the vigorous nature of the species means it bounces back fast from these insults.

Buying notes. Not commonly found at the local garden center, but grown enough so that it can often be located for sale somewhere in the area.

ACER GINNALA (AMUR MAPLE)

Description. Small, rather narrow leaves of a deep, glossy green relieve this plant of the coarseness associated with other maple hedges. Small, fragrant, early-spring flowers, often spectacular

orange-red fall color, and the red "helicopter" seed pairs of late summer combine to give this tough hedge depth of interest. As the undergraduate of hedgeplants, it contributes excitement at useful times, but its stubbornly casual demeanor is not always appropriate.

Cultural requirements. Zone 2. Grows vigorously in full sun or partial shade; full sun is needed for best fall color. Nearly any soil is fine, given that it is well drained. At its best with a moderate amount of moisture, though easily stands up to a summer drought. Also tolerates windy places.

Manipulation. An easily transplanted species, spring or autumn. Cut to within 6 or 9 inches of the ground to assure a wide, leafy base. Prune any time, three or more times a year for formality. However, this plant is at its best as a hedge when clipped once a year to keep it in line. Can be used effectively up to 15 feet tall and half as wide.

Special characteristics. An extremely tough, hardy hedge for informal situations. If you have the dreaded urge to plant the Siberian elm, steer yourself over to the *Acer ginnala* instead. It is every bit as adaptable to difficult situations, more durable, and mostly free of insect and disease problems. When and where the fall color is good, it is very good. Good color is most consistent when the plant is grown on sandy soils, where it is also slower growing.

Liabilities. Autumn coloration is often inconsistent, but usually a good clear yellow is achieved.

Buying notes. The cultivars 'Compactum' and 'Durand Dwarf' are very twiggy and make excellent hedges in the 4- to 7-foot range. They also tend to be proportionately wider than the species.

BUXUS MICROPHYLLA 'KOREANA', *B.* SHERIDAN HYBRIDS (BOXWOOD)

Description. Where it is hardy, boxwood has long been the last word on hedging. Any plant that can be clipped into the shape of a duck and still look good will certainly make a fine hedge. The 'Koreana' variety has small mouse-ear leaves, rich green and semi-glossy in summer, turning toast brown in winter. The Sheridan hybrids have bright shiny green new growth which turns deep green in summer and holds that color well through winter. (They are hybrids between *B. microphylla* and *B. sempervirens.*) The Korean box is naturally rangy and open; however, it forms a dense wall when sheared. The Sheridan hybrids are very dense, usually wider than tall.

Cultural requirements. Zone 4. Boxwoods need a steady moisture supply and soil that is well drained. Mulching is important to help keep the root zone moist and cool. Boxwoods can be grown in full sun, in a protected place where winter winds are not likely to cause desiccation. They do well in all but black shade, too. Boxes are adaptable to a wide range of conditions, provided the roots are kept cool and moist.

Manipulation. The Sheridan hybrids are quite formal and may never need pruning unless you are really compulsive. A light shearing in late summer will leave this hedgeplant smooth and dense for eight months. Plant 16 inches to 2 feet apart in soil that has organic material worked into it. 'Green Velvet' and 'Green Mountain' will grow to about 3½ feet tall and possibly twice as wide. They are slow growers, a few inches a year. Fertilize in spring to encourage growth.

The Korean box has a more open habit and must be sheared to improve density. It can be pruned to narrower dimensions: to 4-plus feet tall and half as wide.

Special characteristics. The Sheridan hybrids are the finest

boxes I know of for northern hedges. These fine-textured, durable hedgeplants extend the range of the classic, classy box into the Midwest and southern Canada.

Liabilities. Boxwoods have an odor that some people liken to cat urine. It's really not that bad unless you stick your nose right in the foliage. The Korean box turns off-color in winter. This habit is tolerated by northerners grateful for any hardy broadleaf evergreen.

Buying notes. These plants are usually container grown and can be planted spring to early fall.

CARPINUS BETULUS (EUROPEAN HORNBEAM)

Description. Michael Dirr, in his *Manual of Woody Landscape Plants*, calls the species "a choice specimen with an air of aloofness unmatched in any plant"; this description is easily applied to a hornbeam hedge as well. Crisp, clean, dark green leaves evenly clothe the well-pruned hedge from soil line to top. A very common hedge in Europe, for good reason. Yellow fall color is common, though sometimes a good orange is seen. The American *Carpinus*, *C. caroliniana*, called musclewood or blue beech, is similar, though it has consistent orange fall color; it is rarely seen for sale.

Cultural requirements. Zone 4. Somewhat adaptable to various soil types and urban conditions; however, the soil should be well drained and have a steady moisture supply. The soil can be acid or alkaline, clayey or sandy, but should not stay wet or dry. Avoid exposed locations, for the hornbeam looks its best in partially or fully protected locations, in full sun or part shade.

Manipulation. A moderately slow grower in all but the most favorable places, a hornbeam hedge needs only two shearings a year, in late spring and midsummer, to stay formal. It can be kept

in the 4- to 6-foot range for years, or can be an excellent hedge up to 40 feet tall and less than half as wide. Plant 3 to 5 feet apart, in soil that has had peat moss or other organic material worked into it. Spring fertilizing is recommended to encourage growth of young hedges.

Special characteristics. This is a hedge whose surroundings should be up to the aesthetic challenge. The clean, even texture of the summer foliage powerfully and quietly enhances the area around. Clear, yellow, autumn color is very nice; in winter the hedge is dense yet uncluttered because even when sheared the branches are clean and fine textured.

Liabilities. Very salt sensitive. Has a reputation for twig breakage in ice storms, but this should not be a problem on a well-shaped hedge.

Buying notes. The cultivar 'Columnaris' makes an excellent tall, narrow hedge requiring minimal pruning. The branches are quite upright and thickly clothed with leaves from a foot or two above the ground. Both cultivar and species are best moved balled and burlapped, with a large ball of soil, in spring.

CHAENOMELES SPECIOSA (FLOWERING QUINCE)

Description. The flowering quince is one of the few hedges that can be sheared at will and still produce a spectacular flower display. There is a wide range of flower color available; white, salmon, pink, orange, or red flowers are followed by glossy red leaves, which then turn a hard, deep green for summer. It makes a strong, impenetrable barrier due to the crowded, rigid branches and thorns.

Cultural requirements. Zone 4. The best hedges are grown in half to full sun. The soil can be of nearly any sort, except wet or highly alkaline. Once established, the hedge is quite tolerant of dry conditions. Also tolerates urban conditions.

Manipulation. This quince is a wide, vigorous plant, so it's unnecessary to plant closer than 4 feet apart. Best kept in the 4- to 6-foot range, as wide as high. For a reasonable degree of formality, you will have to prune two or three times a year, any time. Fertilization should not be necessary. This hedge will tolerate (and return, sometimes) a great deal of brutality delivered by children, footballs, and clippers. Overgrown hedges can be cut back to within 6 inches of the ground for rapid rejuvenation; this also improves flowering and can be made a habit of every few years, especially if you want the hedge kept around 3 or 4 feet.

Flowering quince

Special characteristics. Nothing short of spectacular (or gaudy, depending) as a flowering hedge in the last half of April. Also notable as a stern barrier hedge due to thorns and interwoven, stiff, strong branching. The glossy, dark green leaves are handsome and are held late in the fall, but drop without coloring.

Liabilities. Hard, apple-like quinces are habitually used by other people's children as weapons. San José scale can be a serious pest, especially when the plant is under stress. It is controllable by dormant oil sprays. So tangled are its branches that litter and leaves are liable to catch and become prominent in winter. It is salt sensitive. Sometimes a leaf spot causes early leaf drop in August; apparently this is related to very long, hot summers. Rabbits can damage the bark of young hedgeplants in winter.

Buying notes. It is best to buy plants in bloom: a few erratically placed orange quinces in a line of hot pink will give you an annual headache.

CLETHRA ALNIFOLIA (SUMMERSWEET, SWEET-PEPPER BUSH)

Description. Summersweet is a lovely native plant, under-used as a shrub and very rarely shaped into a hedge. Nonetheless, it is one of the most versatile hedgeplants anywhere. Shiny, medium-sized leaves (to 2 inches) clothe the plant from mid-spring to mid-autumn, when they turn birch yellow (in shade) to bright orange (in sun). White or pink flowers, wonderfully fragrant, cover the hedge from late July to mid-August.

Cultural requirements. Zone 3. Summersweet is extremely adaptable. Sun or shade, even complete shade, is fine. It tolerates wet soil well, in fact takes about any soil condition except alkaline or very dry. This is one of the few hedgeplants that tolerates seaside conditions.

Summersweet, sweet-pepper bush

Manipulation. Transplant B&B or container-grown plants 2 feet apart into well-worked soil with a substantial amount of organic matter (up to 50 percent) in spring, cool summer, or fall. It is often slow to take hold, but once established it is a dependable, medium grower. It should be pruned after flowering, any time between late August and late spring. It flowers on new wood, so pruning through spring should leave enough growth for flowers. Fertilization is useful to encourage young hedges and to maintain mature hedges in less-than-ideal soil conditions.

Special characteristics. Late-summer flowers, bright fall color, and wide adaptability make this hedgeplant special. An excellent cultivar is 'Rosea', which has pink flowers a bit heavier than those of the species. It also flowers a bit later, in August. 'Paniculata'

is also recommended; it has even larger flowers and is a vigorous grower.

Liabilities. Dry conditions make this species susceptible to mites. It also sends up suckers, which have to be kept in check.

CORNUS MAS (CORNELIAN-CHERRY DOGWOOD)

Description. The cornelian-cherry is one of the very best deciduous hedgeplants. Shiny, dark green leaves are crisply held by a maze of strong branches, which, in winter, bear heavy snowloads easily, even on flat-topped hedges. The rigid structure, clothed with remarkably even-textured foliage, lends itself well to formal hedging. The many small, yellow, March flowers are especially good against an evergreen backdrop.

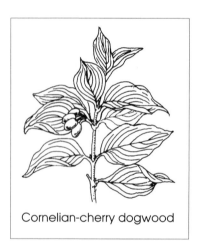

Cornelian-cherry dogwood

Cultural requirements. Zone 4. This dogwood is adaptable to most soils — clay, sand, acidic, alkaline — but the soil should be well drained. Full sun is ideal, but a hedge will stay dense enough with a half day's sun.

Manipulation. Shear or clip twice a year for a formal hedge, in late spring and midsummer. It will need to be as wide as tall, making a solid mass of green between 4 and 15 feet tall as needed. Unless you can locate enough young plants naturally branched to the base, cut back sharply at planting time, placing them 4 or 5 feet apart. Growth rate is usually slow to moderate, so fertilizing young hedges is advised.

Special characteristics. Durability, even-textured density, and lack of serious insect or disease problems give this species the potential to be a handsome, long-lived, trouble-free hedge.

Flowers are welcome in early spring. The bright, shiny, red cherry-like fruits are very nice at close range in midsummer, then are quickly taken by birds.

Liabilities. Though autumn color is often red or maroon, I usually see leaves on cornelian-cherries in New England turning a shaky yellow before dropping. This species is salt sensitive. Rabbits will gnaw, occasionally, at the bark of young plants.

CORNUS RACEMOSA (GRAY DOGWOOD)

Description. The gray dogwood makes a tough, low-maintenance hedge with subtle year-round beauty. The upright growth of red and gray stems is noteworthy in winter, following purple or red autumn coloration. Up close, persistent cerise fruit stalks are present in both seasons, the white fruits of late summer and early autumn having been taken by birds. Plain green summer foliage blends with varied landscapes.

Gray dogwood

Cultural requirements. Zone 4. One of the most versatile hedgeplants around, the gray dogwood grows well in dry to almost wet soils in full sun or mostly shade. Best growth occurs with moist soil that is well drained.

Manipulation. Plant anytime, 2 or 3 feet apart. One shearing or hand-clipping a year produces a dense, neat, informal hedge. Light pruning will leave a good flower and fruit display. Can be kept between 3 and 8 feet tall and half as wide if suckers are removed. Every so often, when it gets too large and woody, it is a good idea to renew the hedge by cutting it back to the ground. Fertilize only when young, or after renewal.

Special characteristics. A quietly classy hedge in every season. The white, early-June flowers are showy but do not shout. Durable, needs little attention, inexpensive. A good supporting actor.

Liabilities. The suckers, while useful in renewing and making the hedge denser, will need annual removal if the hedge is as wide as you want it.

Buying notes. Sometimes this plant is sold under the name *Cornus paniculata*. The cultivar 'Slavin's Dwarf' is finer textured, grows only to 3 or 4 feet tall, and is useful as a low hedge or clipped edging.

CORNUS SERICEA (RED-OSIER DOGWOOD)

Description. A quiet layer of green foliage covers this hedge all summer, hiding the red branches that provide well-timed and long-lasting color in winter. Fall color is ruddy red or purple; the flat, cream-white flowers on informal hedges in May give way to white fruits taken by birds. Pruning of formal hedges eliminates most flowers.

Cultural requirements. Zone 2. Wide range of tolerance. *Cornus sericea baileyi* is a variety, or species, depending on one's source, that grows best on sandy, drier soils; the species *(C. sericea)* is excellent on moist to wet soils. Full sun is ideal, with an evenly moist soil, though the red-osier dogwood will put up with part shade. Extremely hardy, tolerant of most situations.

Manipulation. Because the stem color is this hedgeplant's forte, pruning should be focused toward optimum winter effect. The red is most intense on younger stems, so periodic renewal of the hedge by cutting it back to the ground is a good idea. Though it can be an effective hedge to 7 or 8 feet, and as wide, regular renewal usually results in a hedge in the range of 4 or 5 feet. To

keep the flower display, this rather fast-growing plant should be pruned only once a year, resulting in an informal hedge. This dogwood also makes a formal structure with three or more prunings a year to keep it in line. Once *C. sericea* has grown about as wide as high, removal of suckers as they appear will be necessary. This species can be planted 3 or 4 feet apart in spring or fall. *C. s. baileyi* does not produce suckers and therefore needs less maintenance.

Special characteristics. Red winter twigs are outstanding for more than a third of the year. May flowers are quietly nice, and the summer-fall white berries, though too soon gone to be effective, are attractive to birds. Adaptability to wet ground is an especially useful feature, along with hardiness and durability. Flowers often appear sporadically all summer.

Liabilities. As a formal or semi-formal hedge, the amount of work this vigorous plant requires is a bit higher than average. Plantings under stress, especially chronic water stress, are vulnerable to insect and disease problems, as occasionally are even happier hedges.

Buying notes. Too often, *C. sericea*, *C. sericea baileyi*, and *C. alba* are interchangeably sold as red-twig dogwood. *C. alba* is the Asiatic counterpart to the red-osier dogwood and is similar, except perhaps it is more prone to insects and diseases. I have not seen a hedge of *Cornus sericea* 'Flaviramea', the yellow-stemmed dogwood, and I am not at all sure I'd like to. What I know I'd never want to see is a hedge of alternating yellow- and red-stemmed dogwoods. *Cornus sericea* 'Flaviramea' is prone to canker. *C. sericea* is sometimes sold as *C. stolonifera*.

COTONEASTER LUCIDUS (HEDGE COTONEASTER)

Description. As the common name suggests, this species is at risk for stereotyping, partly due to its many features adaptable to

hedging. Small, green-glossy leaves are located with great frequency along the upwardly arching stems. Fall color includes spectacular variations on orange in mid-autumn.

Cultural requirements. Zone 3. Widely tolerant of soil type; the only soils to be avoided are the heavy, wet sort. A good hedge for seaside conditions. Once established, it does well in dry, poor soils. Full sun is preferable; it is required, in fact, for a complete visual barrier, though a tolerably dense hedge can be grown in half shade. Does well in exposed, windy spots.

Hedge cotoneaster

Manipulation. Plant bare-root, container-grown, or balled-and-burlapped plants 2 to 3 feet apart. Hedge cotoneaster can be sheared any time of year, except in wet weather. A fast grower; shearing may be needed three times a year if formality is desired. Cut entire hedgerow to within 6 inches of the ground to renew old, overgrown, tired, or poorly pruned hedges.

Special characteristics. Handsome, fine-textured leaves and yellow-orange-red autumn coloration are best attributes. A classy, adaptable hedge in cold, dry, windy places. Small but profuse pink spring flowers add quiet color at close range.

Liabilities. Though an excellent hedgeplant in most locations most of the time, problems typical of cotoneasters crop up occasionally. Fire blight is the most serious (to a hedge, especially); during prolonged damp spells, check regularly for blackening branch tips and remove, if found, well below the site of infection, dipping your clippers into an alcohol or bleach solution after each cut.

Buying notes. Mass confusion reigns in many nurseries between *C. lucidus* and *C. acutifolius*, the Peking cotoneaster, an inferior hedgeplant. Horticulturist Dr. E. R. Hasselkus notes that the best way to discern between the two is to examine fruits — *C. acutifolius* has two nutlets, while *C. lucidus* has three or four. However, the hedge cotoneaster generally will have glossier leaves of a darker green than the Peking cotoneaster, which has rather dull leaves. When picking cotoneaster plants out of a garden-center or nursery line-up, avoid those plants with comparatively dull leaves.

CRATAEGUS CRUS-GALLI (COCKSPUR HAWTHORN)

Description. Dark green, polished leaves allow this hedge an imposing presence, even without foreknowledge of the plentiful 2- or 3-inch thorns. The thorns in combination with cacophonous branching patterns make this an utterly effective barrier. Fall color is spectacular, varying from orange to maroon. The white, late-spring flowers and subsequent red fruits are noteworthy on informal hedges.

Cultural requirements. Zone 4, southern Zone 3. The cockspur hawthorn unflinchingly requires full sun; nearly any soil type or condition, except wet, is fine, however. Pollution tolerant. This is a good choice for areas subject to environmental stress, such as drought. Though more or less resistant to cedar-apple rust, a leaf-spotting disease, it is best to avoid planting close to the co-host, eastern red-cedar *(Juniperus virginiana)*. Does especially well on exposed sites subject to wind and harsh sun.

Manipulation. Plant balled-and-burlapped or container-grown plants (which I recommend) 3 or 4 feet apart. Prune B&B plants as usual, and allow the hedge a year to get established before pruning into hedge form. It is best to buy small (2- to 3-foot) plants. Sometimes B&B plants take weeks or longer to leaf out the

summer following transplanting. Plant new hedges in spring only, and mulch with a durable material, as that is a chore you'll not wish to do often because of the thorns. The moderate growth rate can be encouraged by fertilizing. This plant can be sheared, though hand-pruning allows for more interesting texture as well as preserving as many flowers and fruits as possible.

Special characteristics. A classy hedge for trying, as well as luxurious, conditions. Glossy summer foliage is almost as nice as the fall colors of orange, red, and maroon. Impenetrable barrier. Mature hedges are actually dense in winter, too, due to the profuse branching. Tolerates poor soils and exposure.

Liabilities. Thorns can be dangerous (variety 'Inermis' is thornless). A bit ornery when transplanted, so do it in spring. Cut a third out of the top (less if container-grown) and pamper until established. The flowers smell awful and can be nauseating to some people.

Buying notes. Always select bushy, multi-stemmed plants, so that radical pruning is not necessary.

CRATAEGUS PHAENOPYRUM (WASHINGTON HAWTHORN)

Description. The Washington hawthorn makes the best of hedges, for it is an aristocratic plant with four-season beauty. For better or for worse it is hostile, too, due to many long, sharp, polished thorns. As with the cockspur hawthorn, these thorns have a serious potential for injury; do not use this as a hedgeplant near children's areas. Thick, shiny, bright green leaves proliferate on the strong network of branches, and turn orange-red to maroon in fall. White flowers appear on lightly pruned hedges in June; the subsequent bunches of rich red fruits stay colorful well into winter.

Cultural requirements. Zone 4. Requires full sun. Quite adaptable to different soils provided they are well drained — acid,

clay, loam, dry, poor. This species is especially well adapted to sandy alkaline soils. A good hedge under urban conditions.

Manipulation. The Washington hawthorn can be kept narrower than the somewhat similar cockspur hawthorn — about half as wide as tall, and between 4 and 15 feet high. As with the latter, it should be planted in spring, balled-and-burlapped, 2-3 feet apart. One pruning a season, after flowering (save as many flower clusters as possible to have winter fruit), will result in a neat, informal hedge. Two shearings, late spring and midsummer, will make a formal, dense hedge.

Special characteristics. Excellent, dense, impenetrable barrier. Reddish spring foliage, white June flowers, glossy-green summer leaves, bright, dependable autumn color, and clusters of red, pea-sized fruits in winter make this perhaps the most complete four-season hedgeplant around.

Liabilities. The flowers smell awful. Not a hedge to encircle a patio.

Buying notes. If possible, select multi-stemmed plants, so that radical pruning will not be needed.

ELEAGNUS ANGUSTIFOLIA (RUSSIAN-OLIVE, OLEASTER)

Description. Narrow, silver to gray-green leaves of fairly fine texture lend a light but vigorous foliar contrast to varied landscape situations. Excellent when used as an architectural extension from stucco or cement; also useful in seaside areas.

Cultural requirements. Zone 2. Grows well in acid, alkaline, dry, or moist soils; only wet or very heavy clay soils should be avoided. The Russian-olive needs full sun and prefers windy or exposed places. It is extremely hardy, a good urban hedgeplant, and does well in salty seaside locations.

Manipulation. Light soils and regular light fertilization are recommended to help make the hedge denser and keep it healthy. Prune two or three times a year, at any time except during prolonged damp spells. Easily transplanted in spring or fall; put plants 3-3½ feet apart and cut back sharply. Well-pruned mature hedges have a dense, strong branch structure; they may be kept between 3 and 15 feet tall and about two-thirds as wide as tall.

Russian-olive, oleaster

Special characteristics. A tough hedge for difficult conditions — seaside, exposed, cold, drought-prone, or windy. When kept happy, this is a trouble-free hedge. Foliage color is exactly what is needed in certain landscape situations, either to create a gray counterpoint to green, or to pick up and extend the soft gray elements of nearby stones, buildings, or skies. There is no other available hedgeplant with gray foliage.

Liabilities. When unhappy due to poor siting or chronically damp conditions, Russian-olive is apt to be bothered by various insect and disease problems. Erratically coarse winter texture may be offensive to some people. Young hedges can be disfigured by ice storms.

EUONYMUS ALATUS (WINGED BURNING BUSH), *E. A.* 'COMPACTUS' (COMPACT BURNING BUSH)

Description. Both species and cultivar have a naturally dense formality that is accentuated by even proportion of leaf to twig size. They are flexible, aristocratic hedgeplants, whose medium texture and crisp, flat green leaves blend in well with most

landscapes. The autumn color of 'Compactus' is a spectacular, nearly painful red; the species turns intense pink. The flat, corky wings on the twigs of the latter create a complex winter silhouette.

Cultural requirements. Zone 3 (species), Zone 4 (cultivar). Any soil condition, type, or pH is fine, very alkaline or wet soils excepted. Both need full sun for strong fall coloration and maximum density, but the species makes a good hedge in all but the densest shade.

Manipulation. 'Compactus' makes an excellent unclipped hedge when planted 4 to 6 feet apart, but its shape will be round and somewhat open at the bottom. The species also makes a semi-formal un-clipped hedge; it will be of a layered design and blocky. Both are about as wide as high, 7 feet or so for 'Compactus' and upwards of 10 feet for the species. Both also make excellent soft-formal (clip every other year) or for-mal (clip once a year in midsummer) hedgeplants. When sheared, they can be kept in the 3- to 7-foot range. Slow growers, they can be fertilized when young to bring them to a useful size faster. Plant in spring or fall.

Winged burning bush

Special characteristics. One of the lowest maintenance and most widely adaptable hedgeplants around. Showy only in autumn, though quiet strength of character is always apparent. Corky wings on the twigs of the species are a subtly interesting feature texturally, and combined with naturally dense habit make this hedge a good visual barrier in winter. Very dependable fall color on hedges in full sun; by sacrificing that ephemeral brilliance you can have a perfect hedgeplant for shady conditions.

Liabilities. For a few weeks each fall, hedges planted near red brick walls clash badly. The branches of young or poorly pruned hedges can break under heavy loads of snow, but a mature hedge wider at the bottom than top will bear moderate snowloads. Rabbits can injure or even kill young hedgeplants. One can possibly be accused of lacking originality by using the burning bush as a hedgeplant.

Buying notes. Be certain you are buying all of either winged burning bush or its compact cultivar. They look awkward growing next to each other, especially in winter. The compact burning bush is finer textured, open at the base, more upright, and lacks corky wings. These are two hedgeplants you will not need to cut back more than one-third at planting time, so buy plants that are well branched nearly to ground level.

FAGUS SYLVATICA (EUROPEAN BEECH)

Description. If it did not make such a tremendous hedge, it would seem a shame to re-shape this classic tree. The shiny unfolding leaves are the definition of "spring green." In summer they are deeper green, still shiny, and uniformly textured. Coppery yellow fall coloration is excellent. Happily, the aristocratic strength of the tree is not in the slightest compromised by using it as a hedge; it is one of the best.

Cultural requirements. Zone 4. This species flourishes in cool, moist, acid, well-drained soils. Cannot be planted in compacted soils, as it requires plenty of soil oxygen. Intolerant of steady air pollution. This species, more than the somewhat similar American beech, will put up with hot summers provided soil moisture is available. A hedge for full sun or partial shade.

Manipulation. Space hedgeplants about 4 feet apart and, after an establishment season, cut back to a stump a half a foot above the ground in order to force basal growth. An excellent neat-informal

or semi-formal hedge when pruned once a year, in midsummer. Also makes a perfect formal hedge, but this requires three clippings annually. It should be kept almost as broad as high, anywhere from 4 to 50 feet. Fertilizing should not be necessary except on young hedges meant to be tall.

Special characteristics. The foliage is quietly striking in all seasons when present. A classy, trouble-free hedge when its cultural requirements are met. This beech can be kept as a hedge in the medium range for years; after a century or two, however, expect a tall, wide hedge. An occasional case can be made for a purple hedge, in which event the cultivar 'Riversii' is a good choice. Other worthy cultivars are 'Fastigiata', a tall, narrow form; 'Asplenifolia', with shredded, ferny leaves; 'Rotundifolia', with rounded leaves; and 'Roseo-marginata', with tricolored leaves of purple, pink, and white.

Liabilities. Some people do not like the sometime habit of beeches keeping their leaves all winter. To me, it indicates character.

Buying notes. The American beech, *Fagus grandifolia* (Zone 3), also makes a worthy hedge, but it is far less common in the nursery trade. Essentially, the American beech has larger leaves and somewhat lighter bark.

FORSYTHIA X INTERMEDIA (BORDER FORSYTHIA HYBRIDS)

Description. This is one of the better single-purpose hedges, for besides the outstanding early flower show, the summer foliage is crisp and pest free, and the autumn color can develop into a good muted purple. An exception among flowering hedges, the forsythia can be rather formally pruned (that is, clipped several times a year) and still put out a fluorescent flower show.

Cultural requirements. Zone 4. Forsythia grows almost too well. It should be grown in full sun, or at least three-fourths sun. Urban

conditions are no problem. Site away from frost pockets, or flowers may too often be winterkilled to make it worth planting. Flower buds on recommended cultivars are hardy to -15°F. Any soil condition except wet is fine, as is any type, though flowering will be lessened by chronically dry conditions and poor soils.

Manipulation. To allow a maximum of grace, shearing should be done but once a year, after flowering (in May). This also maximizes the next year's flower display. Actually, under most growing conditions, forsythia can be pruned again, in June or early July, for this vigorous plant's annual growth often amounts to well over a foot in a season. Do not fertilize this plant; it needs no encouragement. Transplant any time, placing the individuals 2 to 4 feet apart. Renewal-prune when the hedge gets too woody. Effective in the 3- to 6-foot range, as wide as tall to one and a half times as wide as tall.

Special characteristics. The short-lived but spectacular yellow flower display in April is the only reason to plant this species, if space is available and the view worth it. This is also a long-lived, durable hedgeplant troubled by few insects or diseases.

Liabilities. Can be fairly viewed as a sloppy mess for fifty weeks each year. The purple fall color is not always dependable; sometimes the leaves drop off green.

Buying notes. The cultivars 'Densiflora' (pale yellow flowers), 'Spring Glory', 'Lynwood', 'Meadowlark', and 'Sunrise' (very hardy) are all especially good for hedges.

ILEX GLABRA 'COMPACTA' (COMPACT INKBERRY HOLLY)

Description. The profuse, small, dark green, shiny leaves on slim upright stems are the outstanding feature of this broadleaf evergreen. A semi-formal, broadly conical hedge results from only occasional heading-back of exuberant shoots, and an even-

textured planar hedge of serious formality is possible by shearing. This cultivar bears blackish, pea-sized fruits abundantly, but they are ineffective over much distance.

Cultural requirements. Zone 3. Requires an acidic soil, moist or wet, though tolerates a short dry season. The densest hedges are grown under full to half sun, but a reasonable hedge can be grown in light shade or three-fourths shade. An excellent hedge for the seashore, for it does well in those salty, difficult conditions.

Manipulation. The relatively slow growth can be encouraged by springtime doses of fertilizer beginning the year after planting. Practically formal with no pruning at all; shear once in midsummer for tight formality. Once the desired width is reached (3 to 8 feet and as tall), cutting back the suckers will be necessary, with a lawnmower or clippers. Plant spring or fall, 3 feet apart. Keep heavy snows from punching the hedge down.

Special characteristics. An excellent, fine-textured hedge, especially valuable in wet soils or seashore landscapes. The inkberry is, however, adaptable to many landscapes, especially around rhododendrons, mountain-laurel, and needled evergreens. Quite free of problems related to insects and diseases.

Liabilities. The leaves turn off-colored in winter, usually a brownish green.

Buying notes. Be sure you are buying 'Compacta' and not just plain old inkberry, for the latter is an inferior hedgeplant.

ILEX VERTICILLATA (WINTERBERRY, BLACK-ALDER)

Description. Bright red fruits are increasingly striking, first with the summer's deep green leaves, then against the black leaves produced by a killing frost, and, finally, on smooth gray stems against snow. The growth is quite upright in a well-contained informal fashion.

Cultural requirements. Zone 3. An excellent species for swampy, wet soils, in full sun or partial shade. Soil should be acid with a fair amount of organic matter. It does not need to be wet; in fact, the best growth is realized in moist rather than wet soils.

Manipulation. Though only half, at most, of each season's growth should be cut to keep a good berry display, this hedge can be kept as low as 3 feet by regular renewal pruning: cutting the hedge back to within 6 inches of the ground. Otherwise, it can grow to about 8 feet tall, and as wide. Space plants about 4 feet apart, making sure there is a male plant every six plants or so, to ensure maximum berry production. Fertilize when young, if need be.

Winterberry, black-alder

Special characteristics. Unlike flowering single-purpose hedges, the berries of this single-purpose hedge last from August to mid-winter. Birds eventually take them, usually in a short, noisy period of time around the first of the year. Winterberry's ability to grow in wet soils is unusual and useful. It is trouble free and low maintenance when kept as an informal hedge.

Liabilities. *Ilex verticillata* will send up suckers that will widen the hedge if not removed. In alkaline soil the leaves will develop chlorosis (yellowing).

Buying notes. 'Nana' is a dwarf cultivar excellent for low hedges to 3½ feet, with large fruits.

JUNIPERUS CHINENSIS (CHINESE JUNIPER)

Description. The Chinese juniper has several dozen cultivars commonly available; some make excellent hedges. The foliage is

evergreen, sharp-needled or scale-like (sometimes both forms are on the same plant), and can be blue, silver, gray, or any shade of green. They end up being semi-formal or formal hedges, because either they naturally grow slowly in a compact, even form, or they are normally too loose and open in habit and must be clipped into hedge form. Some cultivars have white or blue fruits, which not only look good and last long, but also attract birds.

Cultural requirements. Zone 4. This species does well in any well-drained soil; it even thrives in dry, sandy, sterile, or otherwise miserable dirt. It is also excellent in hot, sunny places with lots of wind, where it makes a fine windbreak. Even though certain vigorous cultivars will survive, even grow, in partial shade, they do not make good hedges under anything but mostly sunny conditions. A good urban hedge.

Manipulation. Junipers can be pruned or sheared in any season. When possible, prune so that the hedge is wider at the base (this may not be possible with some stubbornly torpedo-shaped types). The container-grown or balled-and-burlapped plants can be planted in spring or fall, between 2 and 4 feet apart, depending on the habit of the exact cultivar. Generally, those with upright branching will be put closer.

Special characteristics. The colors and textures of the foliage make these plants especially useful in dry landscapes. Rugged qualities, including ability to thrive in urban places, dry, poor soils, and exposed sites, are unparalleled by other hedgeplants. The naturally formal cultivars are of low maintenance. On fruiting cultivars the prolific fruits add worthy color and texture, as well as attracting birds.

Liabilities. The tendency of most junipers to lose basal foliage will prevail unless carefully pruned; even then, facer plants may be needed if complete visual blocking is desired.

Buying notes. Following is a partial list of cultivars suitable for hedging.

'Ames' forms a chunky cone, 3 to 5 feet wide and up to 8 feet tall. Heavy fruiter. Bright, steely blue foliage on young plants dulls somewhat with age.

'Blue Point' is a particularly good hedge-juniper because its dull blue foliage is held on a profusion of twigs. Its drop-shaped outline should dictate the shape of the hedge. Can be kept 6-15 feet tall and half as wide.

'Columnaris Glauca' needs annual shearing to increase the density of its loosely held gray or silver-green foliage. A good hedge for tight places, for it can be kept about one-fourth as wide as it is tall, to 20 feet.

'Fairview' displays bright, fresh-green leaves, silvery fruits. Prune every other year for a pleasing dense-yet-graceful habit; a good hedge comes naturally from this cultivar.

'Hetzii' makes an excellent hedge due to its vigorous nature and visually soft texture. Its color wobbles around the silver-blue-green range, with green dominating. The Hetz juniper is a good hedge between 3 and 10 feet tall and just about as wide. Needs annual shearing.

'Hetzii Glauca' is a more upright plant than the preceding, growing somewhat taller with more upright branching. Foliage is a soft blue-green. Shear annually to improve already dense form.

'Iowa' boasts blue-green leaves and many fruits. Every-other-year pruning will leave a pyramidal, semi-formal hedge, to 10 feet.

'Keteleeri' needs annual shearing to improve its rather open habit, 6-20 feet tall and half as wide. Foliage is a handsome, even green; the prolific fruits are large for a juniper. It is resistant to cedar-apple rust.

'Mountbatten' is an excellent hedge-juniper, to about 10 feet.

Very dense gray-green foliage needs little if any pruning to maintain a formal hedge. A good fruiter.

JUNIPERUS VIRGINIANA (EASTERN RED-CEDAR)

Description. Despite its common name, this plant is a juniper, the native equivalent of the Chinese juniper. The red-cedar is much hardier, however, and some cultivars turn a pleasing plum color in winter. The foliage is quite fragrant when cut; it varies from dark to light green, or green tinted gray, blue, or silver.

Cultural requirements. Zone 2. The only requirement as to soil type or condition is that it be well drained. I have seen red-cedar seedlings thriving in cracks in asphalt parking lots. It does very well in dry, sandy, alkaline soils with full exposure to the elements. Full sun is an absolute requirement. An excellent urban hedgeplant. Makes a perfect windbreak.

Manipulation. Pruning can be done at any time of year. Keep the hedge peaked or rounded at the top so it will shed snow without disfigurement. Plant 2-3 feet apart in spring or fall. Size and width depend on the cultivar, but usually the hedge need be no more than half as wide as tall.

Special characteristics. A good choice for difficult conditions: urban, windy, poor soil, dry, or exposed. Under these or better conditions this is a handsome, long-lived hedgeplant of slow to medium growth. It is somewhat salt tolerant as well.

Liabilities. *Juniperus virginiana* is an alternate host of cedar-apple rust, a fungal disease that is not fatal to any host and looks much worse on the susceptible members of the Rose family than it does on the red-cedar. In fact, many people mistake the fungus-directed growths for fruits. However, this is not a good hedge-plant in the vicinity of hawthorns, apples, and crabapples, susceptible members of the Rose family.

Buying notes. A partial list of cultivars suitable for hedging follows.

'Burkii' enjoys a narrow form, though effective up to 20 feet. There is a metallic cast to the dull green foliage, which turns a sort of plum color in winter.

'Canaertii' has one of the deepest green foliage colors of any juniper. Shearing it annually is necessary to encourage density to the normally open habit. It should be kept a third to a half as wide as tall, and is best 8 to 20 or more feet tall. It bears fruit heavily.

'Glauca' has a narrow, columnar form, five times taller than wide; it can get to be 25 feet tall and only 4 feet wide. The name *Glauca* refers to a silvery cast of the foliage.

'Hillii' makes a good hedging subject due to slow growth. A soft summer blue-green gives way to a lovely, distinct plum color in winter. Grows 5-12 feet tall and less than half as wide.

'Hillspire' displays a columnar form that at 20 feet tall is barely 5 feet wide, though it may be kept less than half that size for years. Rather dense and formal by nature, it makes an excellent semi-formal, unpruned hedge. The foliage has a definite yellowish cast to it.

KALMIA LATIFOLIA (MOUNTAIN-LAUREL)

Description. Where acid soils prevail, this is one of the best-loved plants for specimen use, massing, and naturalizing (see Glossary); however, it is also most deserving of more attention as an informal hedge. In fact, in the hands of a careful and patient pruner, it can be trained to near formality. The leaves are a rich, leathery green, elongate and dense. They keep that color all winter in all but the most exposed spots. The June flowers of pink to white are unrivalled by anything with roots and leaves.

Cultural requirements. Zone 4, but hardiness depends on source (see Buying notes). Grows in deep shade to full sun; as a hedge, it is best somewhere between these extremes. Do not expect

absolute visual blocking in deep shade; in full sun it should be in a location protected from sweeping winter winds. Requires a well-drained acid soil kept cool with a thick organic mulch. Do not allow soil to become dry; in fact, mountain-laurel will tolerate situations bordering on wet.

Manipulation. Do not shear into hedge form; rather, selectively hand-prune to desired degree of formality. This can be done once a year, or every other year, in midsummer, after flowering. Once the hedge is established, some pruning will be needed to help maintain basal foliage. This is done opportunistically — when a new shoot appears on an otherwise bare branch near the base, cut that branch off just above the shoot if it is not needed, or, if it is, wait a year and hand-pinch the end bud off in spring to promote branching. Plant 2 to 3 feet apart in spring or early fall. Mountain-laurel hedges are best, as hedges are typically defined, kept 2½ to 4 feet tall

Mountain-laurel

and nearly as wide; but if some basal openness is tolerable, they can be effective to 7 feet. Badly overgrown hedges can be cut back to about a foot off the ground and thus renewed.

Special characteristics. Handsome leaves year round, striking June flowers, and a classy, relaxed character combine to make this a very rewarding hedgeplant. Excellent for shady places and when a hedge is needed to go from shade to sun and look good from end to end.

Liabilities. On hedges kept over 3½ feet, some degree of openness is to be expected at base. Spent flower corymbs are distracting, and picking them off is a sticky, time-consuming task.

Buying notes. Buy plants from a local source. A plant native to Virginia may not be hardy in western Massachusetts. Plants 15 to 18 inches tall with lots of basal branching make the most successful hedgeplants.

LIGUSTRUM AMURENSE (AMUR PRIVET), *LIGUSTRUM X IBOLIUM* (IBOLIUM PRIVET)

Description. As *Thuja occidentalis* is the stereotypic evergreen hedgeplant, privet is to an even greater extent the stereotypic deciduous hedgeplant. It has long been entrenched in the national hedge consciousness — in the mid-1700s it was used in the Philadelphia area as a fence substitute due to the scarcity of wood. Though a good privet hedge is perfectly fine, even nice looking, there are many superior plants around, and not all privets make good hedges. I find the Ibolium privet, a hybrid, to be the best one commonly available for hedging in Zone 5 and protected parts of Zone 4 (particularly cities). Its small, shiny, dark green leaves are abundant on many upright branches. The Amur privet is also a respectable hedgeplant, with its profuse ruddy springtime leaves turning a flat medium green for the summer.

Ibolium privet

Cultural requirements. Zone 5 (4) for Ibolium privet, Zone 3 for Amur privet. Any soil type or condition except wet is fine. They grow happily in the miserable, compacted soils and polluted air of congested cities. Full sun is best, though a half day of shade is tolerable.

Manipulation. Privets can be sheared any time of year, up to three or even four times annually for formal hedges. Twice, once in late

spring and again in midsummer, will keep the hedge presentable. Privets, absolutely, with no questions asked, must be pruned wider at the base than the top to keep them leafy to the base. Loose, leggy, and scraggly existing hedges can be cut back to near the ground to renew, provided they get at least a half day of full sun. They can be kept as low as 2½ or as high as 10 feet, about half as wide as tall. Plant bare-root plants in spring or fall, 1½ to 2 feet apart.

Special characteristics. Fast growing, inexpensive, and adaptable to many soil situations. Long lived with regular renewal pruning. A good hedge for fugitives and others who wish to attract minimal attention. Privets have fairly attractive white flowers, arranged in slim white panicles, which appear for a few weeks in early summer. A smattering can be a dependable feature if the plants are not pruned rigorously until after flowering time; however, they are not the sort of flower that is enjoyed through the olfactory sense.

Liabilities. Stereotypic quality can add boredom to a landscape. Rather high maintenance. Fall color is absent — the leaves fall off in various states of green or yellowish disrepair.

Buying notes. The Regel's border privet makes an inferior hedgeplant, though it is often sold as one. It is silly to pay too much for a privet hedge, so buy bare-root plants, which are inexpensive (often a dozen or so are stuck in a pot of growing medium to facilitate handling and watering, but they are not rooted).

LONICERA X XYLOSTEUM 'CLAVEYI' (CLAVEY'S DWARF HONEYSUCKLE)

Description. This hedgeplant is extremely formal by nature, densely clothed with gray-green, fuzzy leaves. It blends especially well with inorganic materials. Though its natural form is globu-

lar, it is easily sheared into one of the most static hedges.

Cultural requirements. Zone 4. This hybrid honeysuckle grows happily almost anywhere, even in poor, compacted soils surrounded by concrete. It needs full sun. A very undemanding hedge, it is tolerant of pollution and occasional fair catches of footballs.

Manipulation. Clavey's dwarf honeysuckle is an excellent hedge in the 2- to 5-foot-tall range, as wide as high. Yearly shearing, anytime, will keep it extremely formal, the perfect backing for a low garden or edge for a walk. It is also a fine unsheared hedge, one that looks as though it is pruned because of the dense, even growth. Plant 1½ to 2 feet apart, a bit more if an undulating effect is wanted on an unsheared hedge.

Special characteristics. Quiet, dense demeanor is the prime feature of this undemanding, adaptable hedgeplant. This allows it to be uncompetitive and therefore a good blend with other more noticeable plants and architectural features. Instead of a low rock wall, try a hedge of this plant.

Liabilities. Yellow specks on leaves beginning in August or late July are probably spider mite evidence. Weekly hosing with a stiff jet of water will keep the population under control.

Buying notes. Beware of other members of this often weedy, unkempt clan. Common *Lonicera tartarica* (your Basic Honeysuckle) is a nuisance from Day One. *Lonicera x xylosteum* 'Hedge King' makes a fine hedge to 4 feet in height and only 3 feet wide, unpruned. It is finer-textured than Clavey's dwarf honeysuckle.

PHYSOCARPUS OPULIFOLIUS 'INTERMEDIUS', 'NANUS', 'LUTEUS' (COMMON NINEBARK)

Description. Though the ninebarks are often regarded as the quintessential Bland Shrub, certain of them make excellent hedges, for blandness is sometimes a desirable feature in a hedge.

Their fine, even-textured foliage is made dense by shearing; it creates a visually soft but effective barrier. The variety 'Intermedius' is especially dense, and achieves an orange fall color. 'Luteus' is a good choice for that rare situation when a yellow-leafed hedge is appropriate. 'Nanus' is a dwarf form, very fine textured, growing to only 3 feet at maturity.

Cultural requirements. Zone 2. Ninebarks are content growing in almost any sort of soil. They also stay effective as a hedge with less than a half day of sun, though they become splendidly dense in full sun and not-too-dry soil. Urban tolerant; in fact, puts up with most forms of misery well, including windy sites, compacted soil, and bitter cold.

Manipulation. Pruning twice annually, in spring and midsummer, will leave enough growth to produce flowers in between. Pruning three or even four times a year will be needed if a formal hedge is in order. Fertilization should not be necessary on a mature hedge, though it is a good idea to fertilize young and recently renewed hedges. Plant 'Nanus' about 18 inches apart; for the others, 2 or 3 feet is fine. 'Luteus' makes a solid barrier up to 6 feet high and almost as wide; 'Intermedius' is effective in the 3- to 4-foot range, and equally wide.

Special characteristics. The white or pinkish white June flowers are quietly showy. In spring, when the leaves are unfolding, 'Luteus' looks from a distance like forsythia. However, the best features of this group of plants are their extreme toughness and, when sheared, their fine-textured density. They make perfect hedges in chronically hot-dry-then-bitter-cold areas. The fall color is nice, too, where it is dependable.

Liabilities. Since adaptive toughness is the top feature, their flowers, fall color, etc., are usually secondary when compared to other hedgeplant choices.

PICEA ABIES (NORWAY SPRUCE)

Description. Norway spruce, overplanted as a specimen (usually in the wrong place, to boot), finds perhaps its best use as a large hedge. The dark green needles are held for a long time, making this an especially dense visual and wind barrier. It is a tough and durable hedge if its few demands are met. Though the branches arch up, the branchlets hang down, giving an interesting texture for most of the year. 'Densata' is a cultivar, conical and much slower-growing than the species, though it still may attain 30 feet.

Cultural requirements. Zone 2. Any soil is fine, as long as a relatively steady moisture supply is present year round. Norway spruce needs a cold climate, the sort with a winter one does not easily forget. Summer humidity is a plus. Open, windy sites are fine, provided the soil is moist. This hedgeplant tolerates a seasonal period of wet soil. Full sun is best; a half day of shade is tolerable.

Manipulation. The natural pyramidal shape of the tree must be copied for a durable, fully clothed hedge. Prune annually, in spring, when the new growth is finger length. Cut off about half of that with a sharp tool. Do not fertilize this species; it isn't needed. Plant 3 to 6 feet apart, depending on how impatient you are. Expect a large hedge, for it is difficult to keep it much lower than 10 feet tall and almost as wide at maturity. To minimize growth, cut up to three-fourths of the new-growth fingers. Once the hedge has become full and even, electric shears can be used, provided they are sharp and the new growth is not cut off entirely.

Special characteristics. Norway spruce makes a commanding wall of greenery, an excellent formal or semi-formal windbreak. I like to see it kept semi-formal, with sheared sides and unclipped tops. Very good as a border-barrier on large lots or as an architectural extension from large homes or buildings. Actually

achieves grace when grown along the banks of a meandering creek.

Liabilities. Performs poorly in hot, dry, polluted places. It is overbearing when used to shield a ranch house on a narrow lot, unless the object is to bury the house outright.

PINUS STROBUS (EASTERN WHITE PINE)

Description. The blue, silver, bright or pale green needles, tactilely and visually soft, give this species an unusually useful place among the evergreen hedges. It is this interesting interplay between the evergreen solidity and the soft outline that allows this hedge a character both formal and relaxed. Furthermore, it can be kept for decades as low as 2 feet tall or grown as a clipped hedge over 20 feet in height.

Cultural requirements. Zone 3. The white pine needs humid, relatively cool summers, available in most areas of northeastern North America. It is widely tolerant of soil types, wet or dry, but does best in an acid, well-drained, moist soil of moderate to good fertility. It does poorly in air-polluted places or spots subject to sweeping winter winds. Plant so that it gets full sun for most of the day.

Manipulation. A thirty-year-old white pine hedge at the Long-necker Arboretum in Madison, Wisconsin, is 3 feet tall; equally fine hedges of the same vintage are over 20 feet tall. Hedges to be kept low should be pruned once annually; they then will be softly formal. Taller hedges need to be pruned only every other year. In either case, the time for pruning is rather exact — when the new-growth fingers are fully extended in May. Each finger should be cut or hand-snapped to about half of its original length. If you are using pruning tools, they must be very sharp. Once the curved planes that define the sides of the hedge are filled out and most

of the fingers each spring extend beyond the plane, a sharp machete or sharp electric shears can successfully be used. A white pine hedge is best shaped like a church door, peaked in the middle and rounded at the top corners, to help it shed winter snow and allow maximum sunlight to reach the base. Plant new hedge-plants in spring or early autumn, placing them about 3 feet apart. If you do not mind waiting a few years for the hedge to fill out, 6 feet apart will work, too. They are fast growers.

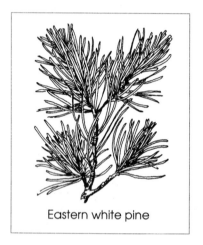

Eastern white pine

Special characteristics. No softer-textured hedge of any sort is available. The needle colors are also unusual and can provide a welcome addition to an otherwise maddeningly green land-scape. White pine hedges require little care once established, giving back far more in return. One of the classiest and most rewarding hedgeplants around.

Liabilities. Snow accumulation can break branches on flat-topped hedges; high winds will do the same to young hedges. White-pine blister rust, a fungal disease transmitted by nearby currants or gooseberries, can kill the plants. Also, they are very salt sensitive.

Buying notes. Due to endless variation in leaf color, select for uniformity when buying. A single silver-blue tree among pale green ones is striking; in a hedge that same plant will look foolish. The fastigiate white pine, 'Fastigiata', is quite narrow when young, but broadens with age. It makes a fine tall hedge, but a frontal planting will be needed eventually, as the branches sweep upward, exposing the trunks.

PRINSEPIA SINENSIS (CHERRY PRINSEPIA), *P. UNIFLORA* (HEDGE OR MONGOLIAN PRINSEPIA)

Description. Tiny, bright green leaves, densely borne on a profusion of upwardly arching branches, appear early and are held late. This is an excellent barrier hedge thanks to another profusion of small, sharp spines. This is a genus that lends itself naturally to hedge use because of its trim, contained growth habit. The Mongolian prinsepia is best as a low to medium-sized hedge, while the cherry prinsepia is taller. The yellow April flowers are not gaudy like those of the forsythia that blooms at the same time; in late summer, they become cherry-like fruits, which birds do not allow to remain long.

Cherry prinsepia

Cultural requirements. Zone 3 (cherry), Zone 2 (Mongolian). The prinsepias need full sun and a well-drained soil. They grow well in windy, exposed places with soil that stays moist. Quite undemanding.

Manipulation. Once established, prinsepia is a strong grower. Both varieties make fine informal hedges, sheared every other year or so to keep them in line. They also tolerate twice-yearly shearing if you want to dictate a shape other than rounded and wider-than-high. Fertilizing should be needed only to speed the growth of young hedges or those growing in poor soils. Horticulturist Donald Wyman recommends when renewing the hedge to cut back only to about 2 feet above the ground. The cherry prinsepia can be kept as low as that, or, more comfortably, in the 4- to 6-foot range, as wide as high. The Mongolian species is best in the 2- to 4-foot range. Plant them in spring, placing the plants 2 or 3 feet apart.

Special characteristics. These are two excellent hedgeplants. They are hardy and pest free, extremely dense and vigorous without being weedy. They hold leaves longer than nearly any other deciduous plant grown in the North. The fruits are a major bird attraction for a few weeks in August.

Liabilities. There is no fall color to speak of. As with all multi-stemmed, twiggy hedges, litter and leaves must be raked or picked out annually.

Buying notes. Both species are difficult to find in nurseries. Lobby your grower for them, for they are not grown nearly enough.

RHUS AROMATICA (**FRAGRANT SUMAC**)

Description. This is a good low hedgeplant for difficult conditions, such as those found between strips of concrete — good as a parking-lot barrier hedge. The leaves are semi-glossy and smell spicy when crushed. They are held very late, sometimes into December in western Massachusetts, and turn a good ruddy-red about six weeks before dropping. This hedge is always informal except for about three days after shearing — a tangled mass of greenery. At close range in summer the fuzzy red fruits are quite interesting.

Cultural requirements. Zone 3. Grows equally well in partial shade or intense sun. Excepting waterlogged soil conditions, any place a weed will grow is quite fine for fragrant sumac. Very good in exposed places, as well as windy, dry, or urban conditions.

Manipulation. This is a stubbornly informal plant, not much good for hedging if allowed to sprawl. To maintain law and order, it should be sheared twice a year, anytime; it is a good candidate for restricted conditions such as those between wall and asphalt, or between asphalt and asphalt. These spots will also help it to

grow *up* rather than out. Plant 4 or 5 feet apart in spring or fall. Unless restricted, it will be wider than tall, 3 to 6 feet tall.

Special characteristics. Unquestionably, the toughness and adaptability of this species are its best hedging features. The fall color, though not consistent, is usually a good red or orange-red. It leafs out early and holds its leaves late. The small yellow March flowers and mid- to late-summer fruits are both quietly interesting.

Liabilities. Heavy snows will flatten a hedge, but it recovers fast with rampant growth.

Buying notes. If available, the cultivar 'Green Globe' is superior for hedging. It is upright and rounded in shape, and less apt to flop about than the species.

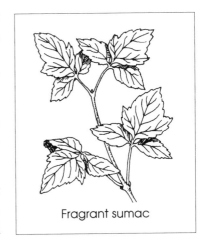

Fragrant sumac

There is a wide range of growth habits in any lot of the species, so select for uniformity.

RIBES ALPINUM (ALPINE CURRANT)

Description. The alpine currant makes one of the most graceful low hedges of all. Profuse, fresh-green, small leaves are held in the center, as well as the periphery, of the hedge, giving it a dense texture. The similarly even texture of the slim twigs in winter is pleasing. This is a hedge that flows well — excellent along curving walks and driveways.

Cultural requirements. Zone 2. This species grows equally well in sun or shade, in any sort of soil, provided it is reasonably moist.

Manipulation. Alpine currant can be pruned (sheared) as often as needed to maintain desired degree of formality. Low hedges,

2 or 3 feet tall and a bit wider, may need up to three clippings annually. The natural half-round shape of the plant dictates the way it should be pruned. This is an excellent candidate for a naturally neat, unsheared hedge — it will form a half-circle shape to about 4½ feet tall. Plant new hedges anytime, placing the plants 2 feet apart.

Special characteristics. Possibly the best-looking hedge for shady conditions. Its neutrality and even texture allow it to fit into varied landscape situations. Alpine currant leafs out early in the spring and holds its crisp green leaves into mid-fall. Extremely hardy, salt tolerant, and of low maintenance.

Liabilities. Heavy snows can squash a hedge, leaving it a foot lower the following year. During hot, dry summers a leaf blight can occasionally cause premature defoliation.

Buying notes. Only staminate (male) plants should be purchased (or, for that matter, sold), as the pistillate form is an alternate host of the white-pine blister rust. The variety 'Pumilum' is excellent for edging or for low hedges to a little over 2 feet tall. It is finer textured, extremely twiggy, and very dense. It also seems to hold its leaves longer, into late autumn. 'Green Mound' is the best cultivar for hedging. It is resistant to leaf diseases, grows to about 3 feet tall and wide, and is very dense.

ROSA HYBRIDS 'BONICA', 'SEVILLANA', 'SCARLET MEIDILAND'

Description. This is a new group of hybrids that show excellent promise as hedgeplants. They have dark green, glossy leaves, a compact growth habit, and spectacular blossoms that begin in June and continue into autumn. The red hips persist through winter, adding striking color to the hedgerow against the snow. This is a hedge that provides cut flowers over an extended season, and gets denser as a result.

▲ Mountain-laurel

◄ Mountain-laurel

© Jerry Howard

▲ Shrub rose 'Robin Hood'

▲ Rugose rose

▶ Rugose rose

© E. R. Hasselkus

© E. R. Hasselkus

▼ Wayfaringtree viburnum

▲ Wayfaringtree viburnum

▼ Russian-olive, oleaster

© E. R. Hasselkus

◀ American holly

▼ American holly

▲ Amur maple `Flame´

▶ Amur maple

▲ Ware dwarf arborvitae

▶ Korean boxwood 'Wintergreen'

▲ Winterberry, black-alder

▲ Firethorn

▲ Winged burning bush

▶ American cranberrybush

▲ Japanese barberry
'Atropurpurea'

▶ European hornbeam
'Fastigiata'

© E. R. Hasselkus

Cultural requirements. Zone 3. In the coldest areas they can be killed back to the roots, and, as they are not grafted, they will grow back strongly the following season. They require a well-drained soil and most of a day's sun, preferably in a spot with some air movement. Like most roses, they prefer a loamy soil, slightly acid or neutral.

Manipulation. Fertilizing in spring, especially after a difficult winter, and again in midsummer with a basic rose fertilizer is preferred. They should be tip-pruned, or sheared, in early spring, and may be cut back sharply to keep the hedge low. Plant about 2 feet apart; they will get 3 or 4 feet tall and somewhat wider if left to their own devices, and tolerate shearing well. They are best as neat, informal hedges. Old, overgrown hedges should be candidates for cutting back severely to stimulate new growth.

Special characteristics. Their extraordinary extended flowering time, neat growth habit, and clean foliage are excellent. They are far less susceptible to pests and diseases than most members of the Rose clan, though extended wet periods can promote fungal diseases of the leaves, such as black spot.

Liabilities. These are new enough to have gathered lots of acclaim and few black marks. Perhaps there are none, but the jury is out.

ROSA RUGOSA (SALTSPRAY, RUGOSE OR JAPANESE ROSE)

Description. Rugosa roses make excellent informal, four-season hedgeplants. They have densely spiny, as opposed to thorny, stems, bearing shiny, rich green, deeply wrinkled leaves that turn a rich dark red in autumn. The flowers appear in early summer, often covering an entire hedgerow, and bloom sporadically throughout the summer into fall. The orange-red hips generally last all winter, adding color and birdlife to the season. Some of the hybrids derived from this species, such as the fragrant white

double-flowered 'Sir Thomas Lipton', bloom heavily in June and again in the fall.

Cultural requirements. Zone 2. Full sun and well-drained soil are definite requirements. This species will grow lushly in pure sand at the seashore; it tolerates polluted air and extreme cold as well. It actually prefers poor soils, slightly acid, though it is widely tolerant of many conditions.

Manipulation. Fertilizing these roses will result in fewer blossoms, and so should be avoided except to increase the growth rate of young hedges. Place new hedgeplants 3 or 4 feet apart. Unclipped, the *rugosa* roses will get 6 or 7 feet tall and at least as wide. Prune annually only to remove the thickest stems (to promote new growth) or damaged or misaligned stems.

Special characteristics. The summer and fall foliage is outstanding. The extended flowering and bright winter hips make these particularly colorful hedgeplants. They are noteworthy for their beauty in wretched circumstances as well as favorable ones, and for their low maintenance and near imperviousness to insects and diseases.

Liabilities. None of these roses is suitable for shaping; they are best left as informal hedges.

Buying notes. 'Frau Dagmar Harstrup' (to 3 feet, pink blossoms darken with the season into fall), and 'Sir Thomas Lipton' (to 5 feet) are excellent.

SYRINGA VILLOSA (LATE LILAC)

Description. In early June this hedge is clothed with blossoms, quite as beautiful but not as fragrant as the common lilac. The late lilac is used best as a large, informal hedgeplant, though even with minimal pruning it is never unkempt. Bold, large leaves are

thickly borne on a great many stiff, even-textured (for a lilac) branches. Flowers may be rose, pink, white, or purple.

Cultural requirements. Zone 2. Full sun is needed for heavy flowering and densest growth, though a good hedge is possible in half sun. Quite adaptable as to soils, but they must be well drained, uncompacted, and not wet. Slightly acid conditions are ideal. A good hedge for windy or exposed spots.

Manipulation. Prune no later than midsummer to ensure good flowering the next year. A fast grower, up to a foot a year — give it space! Due to the large leaves, as well as the growth habits, this ought to be a large hedge, so that the leaves are proportionate. It will grow to 10 feet, wider than high, though it is capable of being kept around 6 feet for quite some time. New plants should be spaced 5 feet apart. Fertilizer is appropriate only to encourage blooming, if necessary. Best planted in spring.

Special characteristics. Profuse June bloom and extreme hardiness are the best features of this lilac. It is a rugged hedge, able to bear heavy snow and temperatures down to -50°F. A good small-scale windbreak.

Liabilities. With no fall color to speak of, this is really a single-season hedge.

Buying notes. The Preston lilacs (hybrid *S. villosa x reflexa*) and *S. palibiniana (meyeri)* are also good hedging candidates.

TAXUS CUSPIDATA (JAPANESE YEW), *TAXUS X MEDIA* (INTERMEDIATE YEW)

Description. There are many excellent cultivars for hedging among the Japanese and Japanese-English yew hybrids, varying in height from 1 to 50 feet. Any other plant used as often as the yews are for hedging would be rightly accused of redundancy; however, a well-kept yew hedge is always appropriate. Deep

green, soft, flat-waxen needles and bright red fruits (arils) are excellent features. The yew can be sheared to rigid formality or hand-pruned to varying degrees of informality. Light green, lacy sprays of new foliage in spring and again in midsummer contrast beautifully with the mature foliage. With the right cultivar and keeper, any shape at all is possible.

Cultural requirements. Zone 4, though the Japanese yew can be grown successfully in protected parts of southern Zone 3. The only unshakable requirement for yew culture is that the soil be well drained. Preferences include acid soil with a steady moisture supply, though most soil types and conditions (except chronically dry ones) are tolerated. The yews put up with urban conditions well, but must be sited away from dry, sweeping, winter winds. They can be sited in full sun or partial shade.

Manipulation. Plant 2 to 5 feet apart, depending on the size of the cultivar. Pruning frequency is dictated by cultivar and personal preference — as little as every other year for informal hedges or slow-growing cultivars in formal hedges, to three times a year for consistent, absolute, planar formality. In the latter case, pruning will be done after, or during, spring and summer growth periods, and once in late summer to clean up the loose ends. Yews can be sheared to look like brick walls, but brick walls painted green are cheaper to maintain. I think the character of the yew is best brought out by hand-pruning the longer shoots to achieve a semi-formal effect; in this case, for most cultivars, one annual pruning after the second growth flush is all that is necessary. The strong branches allow any shape for the hedge, provided the base is a bit wider than the top.

Special characteristics. Enough praise has been given out about the foliage. The yews make extremely durable, adaptable hedges, of medium to very low maintenance. The wide-ranging roots allow successful culture of lawns right up to the edge of the hedge.

Liabilities. If eaten, the foliage is quite toxic to warm-blooded animals. The red flesh of the aril is edible, but the hard seed within, if broken down digestively (unlikely) is also extremely toxic. Both sexes are needed for fruiting, but fruit set is rarely a problem since the yews are so commonly planted. If pruned harshly, as is all too common, the yew hedge looks wan and withered; this sort of treatment negates all reason to plant it. Extraordinary numbers of homes look like they are fronted by a sick line-up of poorly painted, see-through garbage cans. Rodents, especially mice, will chew the bark during certain winters, requiring control measures.

Buying notes. Following is a partial list of recommended cultivars. The heights and widths listed are, of course, advisory. They tell you what the plant has in mind for form; your pruning tells the plant what you have in mind. Obviously things are best when you and the plant have similar ideas.

For low hedges, 1-3 feet tall:

Taxus cuspidata 'Nana'. Excellent. Whorled leaves. Good berry display. Avoid 'Densiformis' (inferior).

T. c. 'Minima'. Good texture.

Taxus x media 'Wardii'. Globose to 4 feet, much wider than tall. Very deep green.

T. x m. 'Chadwick'.

T. x m. 'Brownii'. Hardy hybrid. Excellent, globose, dark green.

For medium or medium-tall hedges, as wide as tall:

Taxus cuspidata 'Jeffrey's Pyramidal'. Very prolific fruiting form.

Taxus x media 'Stovekenii'. Chunky, columnar, no berries.

T. x m. 'Amherstii'. Very dense, one and a half times wider than tall, no berries.

T. x m. 'Hatfieldii'. Pyramidal or columnar, dense, few berries. Zone 5. Perfect.

T. x m. 'Hicksii'. Blocky, flat-topped, a natural hedgeplant. Zone 5.

T. x m. 'Kelseyi'. Very dense, somewhat taller than wide, many fruits.

For tall and very tall hedges:

Taxus cuspidata 'Capitata'. Can be kept one-third as wide as tall, to 50 feet, but easily kept around 6 feet.

Taxus x media 'Sentinalis'. Extremely narrow, tall. Makes a perfect wall hedge.

THUJA OCCIDENTALIS 'GLOBOSA' (GLOBE ARBORVITAE)

Description. The globe arborvitae makes a lovely, undulating, unpruned hedge, 3, perhaps 4 feet tall and a bit wider. The fine-textured green of summer turns to tan and green in winter. The youthful formal growth habit gives way as it ages to a relaxed, sinuous outline.

Cultural requirements. Zone 2. Best grown in full sun, but tolerates one-third shade. Soil can be acid to slightly alkaline, but must be consistently moist. Tolerates seasonally wet soils, too. A cold climate with humid summers (Zone 5 and north) is ideal. A good urban hedge in uncompacted soils.

Manipulation. Though all arborvitaes put up with shearing well, I prefer to leave this one alone. The degree to which the mature hedge will undulate is determined by the planting distance, from little at 18 inches apart to considerable at 3 feet apart. In the early years, fertilizing is a good idea to speed the rather modest growth rate.

Special characteristics. A very low-maintenance hedgeplant, the globe arborvitae needs little care except weeding, and watering during dry spells. Few other evergreens can match the interesting outline of this species.

Liabilities. Careful attention must be paid to the cultural require-ments, or woe will result. This cultivar has great potential to be unkempt, spotty, and otherwise ugly when exposed to dry, hot winds, chronic drought, too much shade, etc. Heavy snows can disfigure a hedge if not knocked off.

Buying notes. There exists an endless variety of dwarf, globular, or otherwise squat forms of *Thuja occidentalis*. 'Woodwardii' is more or less equivalent to 'Globosa'; some say it holds a better green through winter. 'Little Gem' makes a wonderful rounded hedge up to 8 feet tall. 'Hetz Midget' is a special edging or very low hedgeplant with wonderful flat-twisted sprays of foliage.

THUJA OCCIDENTALIS 'TECHNY', 'NIGRA' (ARBORVITAE)

Description. The upright arborvitaes are near-caricatures of hedgeplants, so over-used are they for that purpose. However, they are excellent low-maintenance hedges. Both of these cul-tivars are formal growing, with dense, dark green, fine-textured foliage that is unchanged during the winter. The slow growth and neat habits of these cultivars make them, over time, the lowest-maintenance hedges of all.

Cultural requirements. Zone 2. Like the white pine and Canada hemlock, the arborvitae requires a cool climate with humid summers. The soil can be acid or mildly alkaline, consistently moist, and fertile. Wet places are tolerated well. Two-thirds to full sun is necessary for dense growth. Site away from sweeping winter winds. Keep well mulched.

Manipulation. Shearing this plant can produce a shockingly linear piece of architecture. It seems silly to me, however, not to take advantage of its inherent formality and leave it alone. Place new plants 2 or 3 feet apart, 2 feet if the hedge is to be sheared. These two cultivars are best kept 5 to 10 feet tall and about a third as wide. Pruning can be done at any time of the year.

Special characteristics. Narrow, neat formality makes this plant ideal for most hedging purposes. Trouble free when sited properly and cultural requirements are met. These cultivars are enormous improvements over the species.

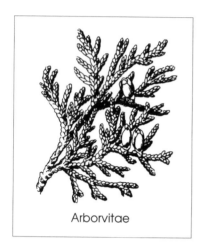

Arborvitae

Liabilities. In some neighborhoods these seem to be the only hedges around; therefore, no matter how well grown, they are boring. A ratty plant when its cultural requirements are not met.

Buying notes. There are many cultivars of arborvitae available; for hedging, most are inferior. Some good ones are 'Fastigiata' (very narrow, tall, must be planted 16 inches apart), 'Douglasii' (narrowly pyramidal, twisted foliage sprays), and some that come under the semi-useless name Dark Green (most are large and vigorous). *Note:* 'Techny' is sometimes called 'Mission'.

TSUGA CANADENSIS (CANADA HEMLOCK)

Description. Tiny, flat, deep green needles and lacy new growth contrast beautifully with the dense, evergreen mass of a well-pruned hedge. This species is to me the quintessential hedge-plant. It can be formal without being stiff, for even when sheared a hemlock hedge has a grace no other can match. It also makes a tremendous semi-formal or informal hedge, and can be kept as low as 3 feet or as high as 50 feet.

Cultural requirements. Zone 3. Requires a cool climate with humid summers, sited away from sweeping winter winds. Plant in a well-drained, moist, acid soil. It may be grown in full sun, light shade (scattered or indirect light), or partial shade (shade

part of the day, sun part of the day). Under the latter two circumstances, it is critical that it be pruned wider at the base. This is not a hedge for areas subject to air pollution or salt.

Manipulation. Pruning the Canada hemlock hedge more than once a year removes much of its charm. For a formal hedge, do an annual pruning in June, after the first flush of new growth has extended. Prune every other year, at any time, for a soft outline. Hedges can be kept between 4 and 8 feet indefinitely. They keep their basal branches well if pruned wider at base than top, so that 50-foot hedges clothed evenly top to bottom with foliage are possible. Hemlocks are relatively fast-growing plants, so fertilization is worthwhile only to speed the growth of young hedges. Plant young hedgeplants 4 feet apart.

Canada hemlock

Special characteristics. The delicate overlay of new growth over the dark green, shaped growth is exceptional. The authoritative green is countered by the soft, tiny, needles for a widely adaptable effect. This is an extremely durable, classy, and fairly low-maintenance hedgeplant.

Liabilities. In extremely hot weather, or if the soil dries out, the tips of young branchlets will die back an inch or two. There is little you can do about the former situation; proper siting or a major commitment to watering will alleviate the latter. Fortunately, in areas where this species is native, these problems are rare.

Buying notes. *Tsuga caroliniana*, the Carolina hemlock (Zone 4), is somewhat similar, though its leaves are a deeper green and are arranged spirally around the branchlets. It is supposedly better adapted to city life, being pollution tolerant. It is a fine

hedgeplant, though never as graceful as the Canada hemlock. Buy unsheared plants whenever possible; they are less expensive.

VIBURNUM DENTATUM (ARROWWOOD VIBURNUM)

Description. This is a quiet hedge-shrub with subtle four-season attractions. Detractors might call it boring, but its subtle nature is precisely why it is so useful. Finely chiseled, fresh, glossy green leaves set off cream-colored, flat-topped June flowers. Though not a dependable feature in all soils and climates, the fall coloration can be orange to red. Native Americans used the stems to make arrows; in winter, their clean, straight habits can be seen. This is a particularly good unpruned hedgeplant for a variety of places.

Arrowwood viburnum

Cultural requirements. Zone 2. Grows well in any soil — wet, dry, or in between. A good choice for difficult spots running through areas with aggressive tree roots such as those of Norway maple. Also a hedge for exposed sunny areas, places surrounded by asphalt, or shaded conditions. It makes its best growth in (mulched) moist soils with at least a half day's sun. A fine urban plant.

Manipulation. Best used as a naturally neat, unpruned or lightly pruned hedgeplant. One selective pruning, at any time, is all that is needed to keep it at a consistent height. This hedge can be renewal-pruned if it gets too large. Plant anytime, 2-3 feet apart. Ideal in the 4- to 6-foot range, about as wide as tall. Suckers will need annual removal (unless, of course, restrained by concrete or asphalt) once the desired width is reached.

Special characteristics. A vigorous, durable, adaptable hedging subject, with few troubles. June flowers and blue autumn fruits add quiet interest in season. Birds like the fruit. Fall color can be spectacular. Excellent for tough jobs such as screening between strips of asphalt.

Liabilities. Suckering can be a nuisance if you expect a no-maintenance planting. I have noticed plants under stress (hot, dry, recently transplanted) develop brown (necrotic) spots on their leaves prior to premature defoliation. The next season they were not evident, however, even though it was hotter and drier.

Buying notes. If buying in autumn, select for good fall color. This will not guarantee good coloration on your property, but will eliminate genetic reasons for the lack of it.

VIBURNUM LANTANA (WAYFARINGTREE VIBURNUM)

Description. This viburnum makes an especially solid deciduous hedge. The leaves are heavily textured with deep veination; the summer color of gray-green gives way in very late fall to rich burgundy. The leaves are often held into December. The way-faringtree is a large hedgeplant with all-season interest, one needing little maintenance and of semi-formal growth habits.

Cultural requirements. Zone 3. This adaptable species is happy in any soil — wet, dry, acid, alkaline — provided it is well drained. A mulch is needed if the soil is dry. To take full advantage of the density of this hedgeplant, plant so that it receives at least a half day of full sun. A good hedge for exposed, windy places if the soil is not too dry.

Manipulation. This is not a plant for the electric shears. Since it is naturally round-formal anyway, if you prune at all it is best done annually in a selective fashion. The leaf and flower buds are, oddly, naked, miniature versions of what is to come; this makes

winter pruning a good way to minimize flower-bud loss, as it is easy to distinguish between the flower buds and the leaf buds. Place new plants 4 or 5 feet apart. This hedge is best kept in the 5- to 6-foot range, and will be as wide as tall.

Special characteristics. The late-May flowers, off-white, are lovely yet unobtrusive. This is an excellent hedge for observing the fruiting at close range: beginning in June, the fruit clusters change from green to yellow, then to red, blue, and finally black, with several colors present on any one cluster. Birds finally take the raisin-like fruits in late autumn or winter. The very late foliage-drop and the excellent fall color are outstanding features. A durable hedge, with few insect or disease problems.

Wayfaringtree viburnum

Liabilities. The leathery, off-green leaves are a bit coarse, so the hedge should be large to be proportionate, which unfortunately limits its use.

Buying notes. Though the species makes a fine hedge, the cultivars are even better. The three most often encountered are 'Lee's', 'Rugosum', and 'Mohican'. 'Mohican' is especially dense, and its fruits stay in the red stage for two weeks at least.

VIBURNUM LENTAGO (NANNYBERRY VIBURNUM)

Description. This is a hedgeplant with many excellent features. The necessary shearing or pruning makes it very dense; the glossy green leaves turn a red or purple-red in autumn. The nannyberry can be maintained as a narrow hedge between 2 and 10 feet tall and less than a third as wide. The cream-colored flower clusters of May lead to fruit clusters that go through a color procession

from green to yellow, red, and blue; these fruits then persist into winter, at which time they attract birds. The leaves are held limply and wriggle in the wind like quaking aspen leaves.

Cultural requirements. Zone 2. This is one of the most widely adaptable hedgeplants, for it grows well in soils wet or dry and of varying pH. It is especially dense in full sun, but also makes a reasonably full hedge in shadier conditions (any but deep shade).

Manipulation. This is a fast grower and will need two clippings a season to stay neat. The flower buds are shaped like a stretched-out lightbulb; when pruning in fall, winter, or spring, you may wish to avoid them as much as possible. Plant new hedgeplants 2 to 3 feet apart, in spring or autumn. Low hedges will need up to three clippings a year, and should not be expected to flower much. In their early years, hedges need be pruned only annually to be tall. Hedges grown too large can be renewal-pruned back to the ground.

Special characteristics. A hedge both culturally and aesthetically adaptable: May flowers, summer and fall fruits, fall color, and interestingly active leaves combine with its hardiness, toughness, and versatility to make a well-rounded hedgeplant.

Liabilities. Sometimes the leaves become mildewy in places with poor air circulation, but this does not harm the plant. Shearing and sucker-cutting requirements do not allow this species to be classified as low maintenance.

VIBURNUM TRILOBUM 'COMPACTUM' (COMPACT AMERICAN CRANBERRYBUSH)

Description. This is an exceedingly twiggy, dense, upright hedgeplant, best used unclipped in its naturally neat, informal state. Small, maple-like leaves are a firm, glossy-green, changing to the wine reds of autumn. Brilliant red berries form in early fall

and persist all winter, often into spring, making this truly a four-season plant.

Cultural requirements. Zone 3. The compact cranberrybush should be grown in full sun. It is adaptable to many soils, but will do best in fertile, well-drained, moist soil. It does not like exposed, dry places, but windiness is no problem.

Manipulation. It is best, once it is established, to leave this hedge pretty much alone. Selective hand-pruning might be needed to even it up every year or two, but do not shear. The natural height of 3 to 5 feet (equally wide) should determine its size. Plant new plants 2 or 3 feet apart, anytime.

Compact American cranberrybush

Special characteristics. A low-maintenance, low hedge. Lacelike, late May flowers give way to the outstanding, persistent red berries.

Liabilities. The vast numbers of twigs catch leaves and litter, which should be raked out annually.

Buying notes. The European native equivalent, *Viburnum opulus* 'Compactum', is much more commonly available. It shouldn't be. It is subject, more often than not, to aphid attacks that badly disfigure the leaves and stem tips. It can be controlled by spraying, which is a bother and eliminates the species as low maintenance. *V.o.* 'Nanum' is more compact than either and very much an inferior plant.

CHAPTER 8

LIMITED-USE HEDGEPLANTS

The following list of hedgeplants, with brief descriptive discussions of their merits and drawbacks, contains those species that did not make the main, recommended, listing for various reasons. Generally, borderline hardiness (usually Zone 5) is the primary drawback. Other reasons might be that the use of the hedgeplant is quite limited due to its cultural requirements; that it requires high maintenance for limited return; that it is susceptible to insects and must be fussed over; or that it has only one short-season reason to be used, such as flowering. All of these plants, however, in some places make useful, rewarding hedges.

ABELIA X GRANDIFLORA (GLOSSY ABELIA)

The glossy abelia is ideally a rounded hedge, up to 5 feet tall and wide. Small, shiny, evergreen leaves borne on a great many upwardly arching stalks set off an August profusion of pink flowers. Even in Zone 5, where it is root hardy, the top may be killed back during harsh winters, though it grows back quickly. Since it flowers on new wood, winter dieback does not affect flowering.

The plant can be kept fairly formal if clipped three times a year, but this reduces the flower show. Once-a-year clipping will leave you with a neat, informal hedge. It should be grown in a protected spot — near a house or evergreens — in the North. Abelia hedges prefer light shade to a half day's sun; in the South they can be grown in full sun. Place new plants 2 feet apart.

This is usually a broadleaf evergreen, with leaves turning a fine bronze in autumn, but it will, toward the north end of its range,

lose leaves in winter. The variety 'Sherwood' is denser than the glossy abelia and grows only to 3 feet tall and wide.

BERBERIS SPP. (BARBERRIES — EVERGREEN)

The barberry clan includes some of the very best and the very worst hedgeplants. By some awful quirk of fate, the worst ones are often used for hedging and the best ones are not well known. The evergreen barberries are generally excellent, their sole drawback being borderline hardiness (Zone 5). They are thorny, with glossy, leathery, rigid leaves, perfect barriers to warm-blooded creatures. They are best as hedges in full sun, but a half day of sun is acceptable. Near the northern edge of their range they should be protected by siting near a building or evergreen windbreak, away from sweeping, dry, winter winds. Their bright yellow flowers are wonderful in May, becoming colored fruits by autumn and often persisting into winter, adding birds and cheer to the winter landscape. They operate best in the 3- to 6-foot range, and as wide, requiring only one shearing a year to be semi-formal. They are adaptable to most soils. It is most unfortunate that these excellent plants cannot be grown beyond Zone 5.

Berberis x chenaultii (Chenault barberry). Zone 5. Wonderfully rich green summer foliage turns burgundy in autumn and is held throughout winter. A prime low hedge 2½ to 4 feet tall. Plant 2 or 3 feet apart.

Berberis julianae (wintergreen barberry). Zone 5. A vigorous hedge-barberry, an effective hedge to 5 feet in height. Winter-burn colors the leaves a light brown in the North. Dark berries are taken by birds in winter. Plant about 3 feet apart.

Berberis verruculosa (warty barberry). Zone 5. Despite its name, possibly the handsomest barberry. It makes a barrier of deep green to 4 feet tall; the leaves are white underneath. The dark purple berries are taken by birds in the winter. Plant about 3 feet apart.

BERBERIS SPP. (BARBERRIES — DECIDUOUS)

The deciduous barberries have several problems. Many serve as weedy alternate hosts for the black stem rust of wheat and are banned in certain areas, subject to eradication. Others are so obnoxiously thorny and crowded with twigs that hedges collecting litter and leaves are allowed to keep the habit, as the average homeowner has no intention of trying to extract the stuff. Worse, it is rare to see a pure Japanese barberry hedge; most commonly it is also a hedge of Norway maple, poison ivy, bittersweet, grasses, and other representatives of the Plant and Litter Kingdoms. Be all that as it may, human beings will continue to plant the deciduous barberries as hedges for mechanical, masochistic, or hard-fought aesthetic reasons.

These barberries tend to have brilliant autumn foliage — orange to deep red — small but profuse yellow May flowers, and bright red berries persisting into winter. They also tend to be free of insects and diseases. Most require pruning to stay formal; more important, they need pruning to correct their natural vase-shape into the widest-at-the-base hedge shape. Old hedges may be renewal-pruned. These barberries can be planted 2 to 3 feet apart; they grow in almost any soil under any conditions, but are not tolerant of salt.

Berberis circumserrata (cutleaf barberry). Zone 5. Interesting leaf texture is added to the bright May flowers, brilliant red fall color, and yellow-orange berries for an effective hedge to 5 feet tall, and almost as wide.

Berberis gilgiana (black barberry). Zone 5. This plant makes an excellent informal but dense hedge, for the profuse, drooping flower clusters and subsequent rich red berries are outstanding. In fall, this hedge is a scarlet line between 3 and 5 feet tall and equally wide.

Berberis koreana (Korean barberry). Zone 5. This species has the same good qualities of the others, and adds vigorous suckering

to make one of the densest hedges around. This habit adds to maintenance, but can be controlled by mowing. Its leaves are quite coarse for a barberry, about 2 inches long. It can be kept between 3 and 5 feet tall, and, with control of the suckers, only half as wide.

Japanese barberry

Berberis x mentorensis (mentor barberry). Zone 5. This hybrid between the Japanese and wintergreen barberries is an excellent hedge for hot, dry, inland conditions. It tries to be evergreen, but gives up its leaves in the north part of its range around Christmas. Its flowers and fruits are not showy, so it finds perhaps its best use as a formal hedge when it is clipped up to three times a year.

Berberis thunbergii 'Atropurpurea' (Japanese barberry). Zone 4. A red-leaf version of the Japanese barberry, useful if one needs a reddish hedge to 4 feet.

B. t. 'Crimson Pygmy'. A finer-textured, smaller version of the above, to 2 feet.

B. t. 'Erecta'. This cultivar has especially upright growing habits, making it simpler to maintain in hedge form. Grows to 5 feet, almost as wide. It is sometimes called the 'Truehedge Columnberry'. It is very dense, even textured, and uniform.

B. t. 'Thornless'. This almost thorn-free, green Japanese barberry makes one more inclined to maintain it by cleaning out leaves and weeds.

CHAMAECYPARIS SPP. (FALSE CYPRESS)

Zones 3, 4. The primary feature of a hedge of false cypress is going to be the texture, for, as a group, these plants display an

astonishing variety. These are evergreens requiring a loamy, moist soil, full sun, and relatively cool, humid summers. *C. obtusa* (below), however, is able to better tolerate the hotter, drier, sort of summer found far from its native coastal regions. Even this species, with the rest, should be sited away from places subject to sweeping winds, unless soil moisture is constant and available for uptake twelve months of the year. Soil can be acid to neutral. *Chamaecyparis* should be sheared only lightly, frequently if necessary, if you are looking for a formal hedge. Most will need only one clipping a year, which will minimize distorting the characteristic textures. This group makes some wonderful hedges when happy, and in fact are fairly trouble free if cultural requirements are met. Plant about 3 feet apart unless otherwise stated.

CHAMAECYPARIS OBTUSA (HINOKI FALSE CYPRESS), *C. PISIFERA* (SAWARA FALSE CYPRESS)

Zone 4. *C. obtusa* makes a beautiful medium to tall hedge — it can grow to 75 feet, so pruning is a necessity. Dark green, scaly leaves are borne on flattened, wavy branchlets. Prune wide at base to ensure retention of basal branches.

C. o. 'Erecta'. This cultivar has a sharply ascending branching pattern, but is usually open at the base. It could be useful in tight spots with a low facer row in front. The leaves are shiny and bright green; it can grow very tall, staying less than one-fifth as wide as it is tall.

C. o. 'Gracilis'. Knotted fronds of deep green foliage are the best feature of this small to medium-sized hedgeplant — 3 to 6 feet tall and two-thirds as wide. It is quite slow-growing and needs pruning every other year at the most. This makes a very special informal hedge of great character.

C. pisifera 'Boulevard'. Zone 3. All members of this species tend to develop dead spots and openness as they age — they're

lovely when young but not very durable. The 'Boulevard' variety (a.k.a. 'Cyanoviridis') has light, steely blue foliage quite mossy in feel and appearance. A dense, upright, and sober hedge to 15 feet tall and only half as wide or less.

C. p. 'Plumosa'. This cultivar, with its airy, light green foliage, is best kept in the medium to tall range by pruning only once a year. This allows the feathery foliage to develop. It must be pruned wide at the base, in full sun.

C. p. 'Squarrosa'. This hedge is best kept in the half-round shape, 4 or so feet tall and somewhat wider. Plant about 2 feet apart. Foliage is a soft, mossy, gray-green.

EUONYMUS FORTUNEI 'VEGETUS' (WINTERCREEPER EUONYMUS, BIGLEAF WINTERCREEPER)

Zone 4. Here is a classy and rewarding hedgeplant, one that may ask for plenty, but gives a lot back. Glossy, fat, evergreen leaves are excellent year round, and set off the orange and red fruits in the fall and winter. This plant clings, being a true vine, to rocks, walls, and trees, or becomes a good upright hedgeplant to about 4 feet when given nothing to cling to. The scale insect can be a serious problem, but is easily controlled by dormant oil sprays. This plant can be hand-clipped or sheared to form a formal or semi-formal hedge in any soil, except those having wet or dry conditions chronic to them. Situate the hedge away from sweeping winter winds and plant the new plants 18 inches apart. Wintercreeper grows anywhere in all but the densest shade. Rabbits gnawing at the bark are a problem in some areas.

E. f. 'Sarcoxie'. This cultivar is similar to the above, but is easier to train as a hedge because it is more upright. It does not fruit well. This variety is also supposedly hardier than 'Vegetus'.

ILEX CRENATA 'CONVEXA' (JAPANESE HOLLY)

Zone 5. This may be the hardiest Japanese holly. It is a top-class

hedgeplant; the only drawback I can think of is its borderline hardiness. It shears easily into very formal hedges, or, when selectively pruned, makes a wonderfully textured semi-formal hedge, as wide as high, 2 to 7 feet tall. This plant prefers acid, well-drained soils with regular moisture supplies. A good urban plant, it furthermore grows well in full sun, half sun, or light shade. Plant 2 to 3 feet apart. While the shiny, bright green, convex, small leaves are the only feature, they are enough — more than enough — to carry the show.

ILEX OPACA (AMERICAN HOLLY)

Zone 5. This is the familiar holly of Christmas. It is another excellent hedgeplant, though its use is limited mostly to areas where it is native, that is, the southeastern United States and along the coast into New England. It should be pruned once a year, in December or any other time. Since it produces berries on new wood, a good crop can be expected under all but the harshest pruning regimens. One male plant is needed for every five to fifteen females, depending on how they are spaced, usually 3 to 4 feet apart. This is a chunky, dense hedge, best used in the 5- to 20-foot range, and half as wide. It tolerates salty seaside conditions well, as well as air pollution. Since it is a species plagued by many insect and disease problems, it should be used only in areas where it is found as a native.

KOLKWITZIA AMABILIS (BEAUTYBUSH)

Zone 4. Oddly, this often trashy plant with the magnificent May flowers makes a hedge that, with shearing, minimizes the inherent problems of form and texture, and enhances the flower effect. It is a stunning line of pink for a week or two in late May, and a plain old hedge the rest of the year. The profusion of fine-textured twigs brought on by shearing softens the leafless winter texture, making it easily tolerable. The beautybush flowers only on old

wood, so pruning should be done after flowering, in June. This also eliminates the unsightly fruits. Plant about 3 feet apart. The hedge is effective in the 5- to 7-foot range and should be pruned wide at the base. Renewal-pruning is a good idea to periodically rejuvenate the hedge. There are few insect or disease problems.

Beautybush

LARIX DECIDUA (EUROPEAN LARCH), *L. LARICINA* (AMERICAN LARCH, TAMARACK)

Zone 2. For hedging purposes, the American and European larches are similar, for they are needle-bearing yet deciduous, with a clear to golden yellow fall color. The early spring foliage of the freshest green is memorable. The American larch (tamarack) is less adaptable than its European counterpart, but is excellent on wet or boggy soils in areas to which it is native, namely, the northern tier states and northern and eastern Canada. Extreme hardiness and tolerance of wet soil conditions are the best attributes of these species, although their best growth is made on better-drained soils. The European larch easily tolerates dry soils, as well. These are plants for large hedges, 6 to 20 feet tall. Plant 3 feet apart. The tamarack can be half as wide as tall, the European larch rather wider. Prune in midsummer. They require full sun. *L. d.* 'Fastigiata' is a very narrow form and occasionally finds good use.

PINUS MUGO (MUGHO PINE)

Zone 2. When this plant is grown well, there is no finer hedge. Unfortunately, when planted in the concentration required in a hedge, scale problems are likely unless controlled by dormant oil

spraying. This pine has many varieties, often not well marked in the trade. The variety 'mugo' is best for hedging. It is excellent in the 3- to 5-foot range, half-round shape, wider than high, and can be planted about 3 feet apart. As with other pines, pruning consists of cutting or snapping the new-growth fingers in May. It should be grown in full sun in any well-drained soil that is not subject to prolonged drying.

PINUS RESINOSA (RED PINE)

Zone 2. This is an extremely tough, hardy hedgeplant for the far North. It flourishes in sterile, dry, sandy soils berated by bitter cold or extreme heat, wind, and exposure. It can be grown as a hedge in the 4- to 20-foot range, as wide as tall when small, and maybe half as wide when tall (over 12 feet). Prune in spring or early summer by breaking the new-growth fingers in two, or cutting them cleanly. The hedge must be shaped so that it is wider at the base than the top, and so that the top will shed snow easily. The brittle, long (6-inch) needles are dark green in summer, often turning paler in winter. This is a dependable, low-maintenance hedge that looks good under adversity.

PYRACANTHA COCCINEA (FIRETHORN)

Zone 6; some cultivars Zone 5. This is a rather demanding hedge, but the orange-red fruit display of fall and winter makes it worthwhile to some. Firethorn hedges require frequent pruning to keep reasonably neat, and the small-but-cruel spines make it risky business. It is obviously an excellent barrier hedge. The evergreen leaves will turn brown when exposed to win-

Firethorn

ter wind and too much winter sun under dry conditions, and tend to drop altogether near the northern edge of its range. This hedge grows well in partial shade, and takes to most soils, even those tending toward wet. The flat, off-white, June flower clusters nearly cover the plant, but somehow never seem as showy as they ought to be. The cultivars 'Chadwick', 'Kasan', 'Lalandi', 'Mohave', and 'Wyattii' are all hardy in Zone 5. There are several insect and disease problems affecting the firethorn; the cultivar 'Mohave' is resistant to the most serious two: fire blight and scab. Luckily, none of the diseases is limiting.

SYRINGA X CHINENSIS (CHINESE LILAC)

Zone 4. The fragrant, late-May flowers are really the only reason to use the Chinese lilac as a hedge, though it behaves itself well enough the rest of the year. The leaf texture is a bit finer than that

Chinese lilac

of the common lilac, and it tends to be better branched near the ground. It also does not sucker. The uniform leaves are exhibited in peak form on a hedge, making it very even textured and able to fit into varied landscapes. As with the common lilac, the foliage is bound to get mildewed during humid summers. This is a hedgeplant to be kept in the 3- to 7-foot range. One pruning after flowering will keep it neat; another in midsummer will result in a fairly formal hedge. The Chinese lilac tolerates a wide variety of soil and climatic conditions, but should be planted in full sun, about 3 feet apart. There are purple- and red-flowering varieties.

CHAPTER 9

HEDGEPLANT SPECIAL FEATURES

APPROXIMATE MONTH OF BLOOM
(Asterisks denote plants with showy or noticeable flowers —
the more asterisks, the more prominent the display.)

MARCH:
Buxus microphylla koreana (Korean box)
Rhus aromatica (fragrant sumac)

APRIL:
Acer ginnala (Amur maple)
Carpinus betulus (European hornbeam)
Chaenomeles speciosa (flowering quince)***
Cornus mas (cornelian-cherry dogwood)*
Forsythia x intermedia (border forsythia)***
Prinsepia sinensis (cherry prinsepia)
P. uniflora (Mongolian prinsepia)

MAY:
Berberis spp. (barberries)**
Cornus sericea (red-osier dogwood)*
Cotoneaster lucidus (hedge cotoneaster)
Crataegus crus-galli (cockspur hawthorn)**
Euonymus alatus (burning bush)
Fagus sylvatica (European beech)
Lonicera x xylosteum (Clavey's dwarf honeysuckle)
Syringa chinensis (Chinese lilac)***
Viburnum lantana (wayfaringtree viburnum)*
V. lentago (nannyberry)*
V. trilobum (cranberrybush viburnum)*

JUNE:
Cornus racemosa (gray dogwood)*
Crataegus phaenopyrum (Washington hawthorn)**
Euonymus fortunei 'Vegetus' (wintercreeper)

Ilex crenata 'Convexa' (Japanese holly)
I. glabra 'Compacta' (inkberry holly)
I. opaca (American holly)
Kalmia latifolia (mountain-laurel)***
Kolkwitzia amabilis (beautybush)***
Ligustrum spp. (privet)
Pyracantha coccinea (firethorn)**
Rosa spp. and hybrids (rose)***
Syringa villosa (late lilac)***
Viburnum dentatum (arrowwood viburnum)*

JULY:
Abelia x grandiflora (glossy abelia)***

AUGUST:
Clethra alnifolia (summersweet, sweet-pepper bush)**

HEDGEPLANTS WITH POISONOUS PARTS

Buxus spp. (boxwoods): leaves, twigs
Euonymus spp. (burning bush, wintercreeper): bark, fruit, twigs
Ilex spp. (hollies): berries, leaves
Kalmia latifolia (mountain-laurel): bark, flowers, fruit, leaves
Ligustrum spp. (privets): berries, leaves
Taxus spp. (yews): bark, leaves, twigs, seed

BIRD-ATTRACTING HEDGEPLANTS

Acer ginnala (Amur maple)
Berberis spp. (barberries)
Cornus mas (cornelian-cherry dogwood)
C. racemosa (gray dogwood)
C. sericea (red-osier dogwood)
Cotoneaster lucidus (hedge cotoneaster)
Crataegus crus-galli (cockspur hawthorn)

C. phaenopyrum (Washington hawthorn)
Eleagnus angustifolia (Russian-olive, oleaster)
Euonymus fortunei 'Vegetus' (wintercreeper)
Ilex crenata 'Convexa' (Japanese holly)
I. glabra 'Compacta' (inkberry holly)
I. opaca (American holly)
I. verticillata (winterberry)
Juniperus chinensis 'Ames', 'Fairview', 'Hetzii', 'Iowa', 'Keteleeri'
(Chinese juniper)
J. virginiana 'Canaertii' (eastern red-cedar)
Prinsepia sinensis (cherry prinsepia)
P. uniflora (Mongolian prinsepia)
Pyracantha coccinea (firethorn)
Rhus aromatica (fragrant sumac)
Rosa 'Meidiland' (Meidiland roses)
Rosa rugosa (rugose rose)
Viburnum spp. (viburnums)

EVERGREEN HEDGES

BROADLEAF:
Abelia x grandifolia (glossy abelia)
Berberis x chenaultii (Chenault barberry)
B. julianae (wintergreen barberry)
B. verruculosa (warty barberry)
Buxus microphylla 'Koreana' (Korean box)
Buxus Sheridan hybrids (boxwood)
Euonymus fortunei 'Vegetus' (wintercreeper)
Ilex crenata 'Convexa' (Japanese holly)
I. glabra 'Compacta' (inkberry holly)
I. opaca (American holly)
Kalmia latifolia (mountain-laurel)
Pyracantha coccinea (firethorn)

NEEDLE:
Picea abies (Norway spruce)

Pinus mugo (mugho pine)
P. resinosa (red pine)
P. strobus (eastern white pine)
Taxus spp. (yews)
Tsuga spp. (hemlocks)

SCALE- OR AWL-SHAPED LEAF:
Juniperus spp. (junipers)
Thuja occidentalis cvs. (arborvitae)

HEDGEPLANTS WITH FALL COLOR

Abelia x grandifolia (glossy abelia): bronze (evergreen)
Acer ginnala (Amur maple): yellow, orange, red
Berberis x chenaultii (Chenault barberry): burgundy (evergreen)
B. circumserrata (cutleaf barberry): red
B. gilgiana (black barberry): scarlet
B. x mentorensis (mentor barberry): red, brown
Carpinus betulus (European hornbeam): yellow
Clethra alnifolia (summersweet, sweet-pepper bush): yellow to orange
Cornus racemosa (gray dogwood): purple
C. sericea (red-osier dogwood): red, purple
Cotoneaster lucidus (hedge cotoneaster): orange
Crataegus crus-galli (cockspur hawthorn): orange to maroon
C. phaenopyrum (Washington hawthorn): orange to deep red
Euonymus alatus (burning bush): pink
E. a. 'Compactus' (compact burning bush): red
Fagus sylvatica (European beech): yellow to copper
Forsythia x intermedia (border forsythia): purple, green
Ilex verticillata (winterberry): black
Juniperus virginiana 'Burkii', 'Hillii' (eastern red-cedar): plum (evergreen)
Larix decidua (European larch): yellow
Physocarpus opulifolius (ninebark): yellow, brown
Rhus aromatica (fragrant sumac): ruddy red, green
Rosa rugosa (rugose rose): deep red
Viburnum dentatum (arrowwood viburnum): yellow, orange, red

V. lantana (wayfaringtree viburnum): burgundy
V. lentago (nannyberry): red, purple
V. trilobum 'Compactum' (compact American cranberrybush): deep red

HEDGES FOR FLOWERING

Berberis spp. (barberries): yellow, drooping
Chaenomeles speciosa (flowering quince): white, pink, red, orange
Clethra alnifolia (summersweet): white, pink
Cornus spp. (dogwoods): white, flat-topped
Crataegus spp. (hawthorns): white, flat-topped
Forsythia x intermedia (border forsythia): yellow
Kalmia latifolia (mountain-laurel): pink (buds), white, maroon
Kolkwitzia amabilis (beautybush): pink
Physocarpus opulifolius 'Intermedius' (ninebark): white, small
Pyracantha coccinea (firethorn): off-white, flat-topped
Rosa 'Meidiland' (Meidiland roses): red, white, pink
Rosa rugosa (rugose rose): pink and white
Syringa spp. (lilacs): white, rose, purples
Viburnum spp. (viburnums): white, flat-topped

HEDGES FOR COLORFUL FRUITS

Acer ginnala (Amur maple): red samara
Berberis circumserrata (cutleaf barberry): reddish yellow
B. gilgiana (black barberry): rich red
B. koreana (Korean barberry): bright red
B. thunbergii cvs. (Japanese barberry): red
Cornus mas (cornelian-cherry dogwood): red, edible
C. racemosa (gray dogwood): white, red pedicels
C. sericea (red-osier dogwood): white
Crataegus crus-galli (cockspur hawthorn): red
C. phaenopyrum (Washington hawthorn): red

Euonymus fortunei 'Vegetus' (wintercreeper): red and orange

Ilex opaca (American holly): red

I. verticillata (winterberry): red

Juniperus chinensis 'Ames', 'Iowa', 'Keteleeri' (Chinese juniper): blue dusted with white

Juniperus virginiana 'Canaertii' (eastern red-cedar): blue dusted with white

Prinsepia sinensis (cherry prinsepia): red

P. uniflora (Mongolian prinsepia): bluish red

Pyracantha coccinea (firethorn): red orange

Rhus aromatica (fragrant sumac): soft red

Rosa 'Meidiland' (Meidiland roses): red

Rosa rugosa (rugose rose): red orange

Taxus cuspidata 'Nana', 'Jeffrey's Pyramidal' (Japanese yew): red and black

Taxus x media 'Kelseyi', 'Hicksii' (intermediate yew): red and black

Viburnum dentatum (arrowwood viburnum): blue

V. lantana (wayfaringtree viburnum): red, blue, black

V. lentago (nannyberry): red, blue, black

V. trilobum 'Compactum' (compact American cranberrybush): red

HEDGEPLANTS FOR MINIMAL MAINTENANCE

(Note: Any hedge will require a minimum of 1-5 hours of attention annually.)

Berberis x chenaultii (Chenault barberry)

B. julianae (wintergreen barberry)

B. verruculosa (warty barberry)

Buxus microphylla koreana (Korean box)

Buxus Sheridan hybrids (boxwood)

Carpinus betulus (European hornbeam)

Chamaecyparis obtusa 'Erecta', 'Gracilis' (Hinoki false cypress)

C. pisifera 'Boulevard', 'Plumosa', 'Squarrosa' (Sawara false cypress)

Clethra alnifolia (summersweet, sweet-pepper bush)

Cornus mas (cornelian-cherry dogwood)

C. racemosa (gray dogwood)

C. sericea (red-osier dogwood)
Crataegus phaenopyrum (Washington hawthorn)
Euonymus alatus (burning bush)
E. a. 'Compactus' (compact burning bush)
Ilex crenata 'Convexa' (Japanese holly)
I. glabra 'Compacta' (inkberry holly)
Juniperus chinensis 'Ames', 'Fairview', 'Mountbatten' (Chinese juniper)
J. virginiana 'Hillii', 'Hillspire' (eastern red-cedar)
Lonicera x xylosteum 'Claveyi', 'Hedge King' (dwarf honeysuckle)
Picea abies (Norway spruce)
Pinus resinosa (red pine)
P. strobus (eastern white pine)
Prinsepia sinensis (cherry prinsepia)
P. uniflora (Mongolian prinsepia)
Rhus aromatica (fragrant sumac)
Ribes alpinum (alpine currant)
Rosa 'Meidiland' (Meidiland roses)
Rosa rugosa (rugose rose)
Syringa x chinensis (Chinese lilac)
S. villosa (late lilac)
Taxus cuspidata cvs. (Japanese yew)
T. x media cvs. (intermediate yew)
Thuja occidentalis 'Globosa', 'Nigra', 'Techny' (arborvitae)
Tsuga canadensis (Canada hemlock)
T. caroliniana (Carolina hemlock)
Viburnum dentatum (arrowwood viburnum)
V. lantana (wayfaringtree viburnum)
V. trilobum 'Compactum' (compact American cranberrybush)

HEDGEPLANTS WITH OTHER-THAN-GREEN FOLIAGE

Berberis thunbergii 'Atropurpurea' (Japanese barberry): red-purple
Chamaecyparis pisifera 'Boulevard' (Sawara false cypress): steely blue
C. p. 'Squarrosa': gray
Eleagnus angustifolia (Russian-olive, oleaster): gray

Fagus sylvatica 'Riversii' (European beech): purple
F. s. 'Roseo-marginata': purple, pink, and white (tricolor)
Juniperus chinensis 'Ames', 'Blue Point' (Chinese juniper): steely blue
J. c. 'Hetzii Glauca': silver-blue
J. c. 'Hetzii', 'Iowa': blue-green
J. c. 'Mountbatten': gray-green
J. virginiana 'Burkii', 'Hillii' (eastern red-cedar): plum (winter only)
J. v. 'Burkii': steely blue
J. v. 'Glauca': silver-blue
J. v. 'Hillii': blue-green (summer only)
Lonicera x xylosteum 'Claveyi', 'Hedge King' (dwarf honeysuckle): gray-green
Physocarpus opulifolius 'Luteus' (ninebark): yellow
Pinus strobus (eastern white pine) — some: blue-green
Viburnum lantana (wayfaringtree viburnum): gray-green

HEDGEPLANTS TOLERANT OF SALT

(No hedgeplant *likes* salt, but a few tolerate soil poisoned by salt —
next to driveways, for instance — or salt spray from the ocean or
a busy northern street.)

Clethra alnifolia (summersweet, sweet-pepper bush)
Eleagnus angustifolia (Russian-olive, oleaster)
Ilex glabra 'Compacta' (inkberry holly)
I. opaca (American holly)
Juniperus virginiana (eastern red-cedar)
Rhus aromatica (fragrant sumac)
Ribes alpinum (alpine currant
Rosa rugosa (rugose rose)

HEDGEPLANTS FOR SHADE

	Half Day	Three-fourths Day	Light Shade	Full Shade
Abelia x grandiflora (glossy abelia)	x	x	x	
Acanthopanax sieboldianus (fiveleaf aralia)	x	x	x	
Acer ginnala (Amur maple)	x			
Berberis spp. (barberries) — evergreen	x			
Buxus microphylla koreana (Korean box)	x	x	x	
Buxus Sheridan hybrids (boxwood)	x	x		
Carpinus betulus (European hornbeam)	x			
Chaenomeles speciosa (flowering quince)	x			
Clethra alnifolia (summersweet)	x	x	x	x
Cornus racemosa (gray dogwood)	x	x	x	
C. sericea (red-osier dogwood)	x			
Euonymus alatus (burning bush)	x	x	x	
E. fortunei 'Sarcoxie', 'Vegetus' (wintercreeper)	x	x	x	
Ilex crenata 'Convexa' (Japanese holly)	x	x	x	
I. glabra 'Compacta' (inkberry holly)	x	x	x	
I. opaca (American holly)	x	x	x	
Kalmia latifolia (mountain-laurel)	x	x	x	x
Physocarpus opulifolius (ninebark)	x			
Rhus aromatica (fragrant sumac)	x	x	x	
Ribes alpinum (alpine currant)	x	x	x	x
Taxus cvs. (Japanese yews)	x	x	x	
Thuja occidentalis cvs. (arborvitae)	x			
Tsuga canadensis (Canada hemlock)	x	x	x	
T. caroliniana (Carolina hemlock)	x	x	x	
Viburnum dentatum (arrowwood viburnum)	x	x	x	
V. lantana (wayfaringtree viburnum)	x			
V. lentago (nannyberry)	x	x	x	
V. trilobum 'Compactum' (compact American cranberrybush)	x			

HEDGEPLANTS SIX FEET AND UP
(Can be kept lower if desired.)

	Height Range
Acer ginnala (Amur maple)	6-15
Carpinus betulus (European hornbeam)	6-30
C. b. 'Fastigiata'	10-30
Chamaecyparis obtusa (Hinoki false cypress)	6-25
C. o. 'Erecta'	10-25
C. pisifera 'Boulevard' (Sawara false cypress)	6-20
C. p. 'Plumosa'	6-20
Cornus mas (cornelian-cherry dogwood)	6-15
Crataegus crus-galli (cockspur hawthorn)	6-15
C. phaenopyrum (Washington hawthorn)	6-20
Eleagnus angustifolia (Russian-olive, oleaster)	6-15
Fagus sylvatica (European beech)	6-40
Ilex opaca (American holly)	6-15
Juniperus chinensis 'Fairview' (Chinese juniper)	6-15
J. c. 'Hetzii Glauca'	6-15
J. c. 'Keteleeri'	6-20
J. c. 'Mountbatten'	6-12
J. virginiana 'Burkii' (eastern red-cedar)	6-20
J. v. 'Canaertii'	6-20
J. v. 'Glauca'	6-15
J. v. 'Hillii'	6-15
J. v. 'Hillspire'	6-20
Larix decidua (European larch)	6-30
Picea abies (Norway spruce)	10-40
Pinus resinosa (red pine)	6-20
P. strobus (eastern white pine)	6-30
Syringa villosa (late lilac)	6-12
Taxus cuspidata 'Capitata' (Japanese yew)	6-30
T. x media 'Hatfieldii' (intermediate yew)	6-12
T. x m. 'Hicksii'	6-20
T. x m. 'Sentinalis'	10-25
Thuja occidentalis 'Techny' (arborvitae)	6-15
T. o. 'Nigra'	6-20
Tsuga canadensis (Canada hemlock)	6-40
T. caroliniana (Carolina hemlock)	6-40
Viburnum lentago (nannyberry)	6-15

HEDGES FOR TIGHT PLACES

(Plants listed can be kept at least three times taller than they are wide.)

	Ratio
Buxus microphylla koreana (Korean box)	4:1
Carpinus betulus 'Columnaris' (European hornbeam)	4:1
Chamaecyparis obtusa 'Erecta' (Hinoki false cypress)	4:1
C. pisifera 'Boulevard' (Sawara false cypress)	3:1
Crataegus phaenopyrum (Washington hawthorn)	4:1
Juniperus chinensis 'Columnaris Glauca' (Chinese juniper)	5:1
J. c. 'Fairview'	5:1
J. c. 'Mountbatten'	4:1
J. virginiana 'Burkii' (eastern red-cedar)	3:1
J. v. 'Glauca'	5:1
J. v. 'Hillspire'	4:1
Ligustrum x ibolium (Ibolium privet)	4:1
Taxus x media 'Sentinalis' (intermediate yew)	5:1
Thuja occidentalis 'Techny' (arborvitae)	4:1
T. o. 'Fastigiata'	8:1
T. o. 'Nigra'	3:1
Viburnum lentago (nannyberry)	4:1

HEDGES FOR URBAN CONDITIONS

Acanthopanax sieboldianus (fiveleaf aralia)
Acer ginnala (Amur maple)
Berberis spp. (barberries)—deciduous and evergreen
Buxus microphylla koreana (Korean box)
Cornus racemosa (gray dogwood)
Crataegus spp. (hawthorns)
Eleagnus angustifolia (Russian-olive, oleaster)
Euonymus spp. (burning bush)—deciduous and evergreen
Forsythia x intermedia (border forsythia)
Ilex spp. (hollies)
Juniperus spp. (junipers)
Kolkwitzia amabilis (beautybush)
Ligustrum x ibolium (Ibolium privet)

Lonicera x xylosteum 'Claveyi', 'Hedge King' (dwarf honeysuckle)
Physocarpus opulifolius 'Intermedius' (ninebark)
Prinsepia spp. (prinsepias)
Pyracantha coccinea (firethorn)
Rhus aromatica (fragrant sumac)
Ribes alpinum (alpine currant)
Rosa rugosa (rugose rose)
Taxus spp. (yews)

HEDGEPLANTS TOLERANT OF WET SOIL

Acanthopanax sieboldianus (fiveleaf aralia)
Clethra alnifolia (summersweet)
Cornus racemosa (gray dogwood)
C. sericea (red-osier dogwood)
Ilex glabra 'Compacta' (inkberry holly)
I. verticillata (winterberry)
Kalmia latifolia (mountain-laurel)
Larix laricina (American larch)
Thuja spp. (arborvitae)
Viburnum dentatum (arrowwood viburnum)
V. lentago (wayfaringtree viburnum)

HEDGEPLANTS FOR WINDY, DRY, EXPOSED CONDITIONS

Acer ginnala (Amur maple)
Berberis thunbergii cvs. (Japanese barberry)
Cotoneaster lucidus (hedge cotoneaster)
Crataegus crus-galli (cockspur hawthorn)
Eleagnus angustifolia (Russian-olive, oleaster)
Juniperus spp. (junipers)
Lonicera x xylosteum 'Claveyi', 'Hedge King' (dwarf honeysuckle)

Physocarpus opulifolius 'Intermedius' (ninebark)
Pinus resinosa (red pine)
Prinsepia spp. (prinsepias)
Syringa villosa (late lilac)

HEDGEPLANTS COLORFUL IN WINTER

Berberis x chenaultii (Chenault barberry): yellow, red berries
B. gilgiana (black barberry): red berries
B. koreana (Korean barberry): red berries
B. thunbergii cvs. (Japanese barberry): red berries
Cornus racemosa (gray dogwood): red pedicels, reddish twigs
C. sericea (red-osier dogwood): red twigs
Crataegus phaenopyrum (Washington hawthorn): red, orange berries
Ilex opaca (American holly): red berries
I. verticillata (winterberry): red berries
Pyracantha coccinea (firethorn): red, orange berries
Rosa 'Meidiland' (Meidiland roses): red berries
Rosa rugosa (rugose rose): red orange berries, reddish twigs
Viburnum trilobum 'Compactum' (compact American cranberrybush): red
berries

GLOSSARY

Adventitious: A bud produced somewhere other than a node.

Apical: The point farthest from the roots along a shoot.

Balled-and-burlapped (B&B): Dug plants, dormant or active, with the soil surrounding the root ball wrapped in burlap or a synthetic mesh.

Bare-root: Dormant plants dug without soil around roots and kept under high humidity and cool temperatures until sold. Also, formerly dormant bare-root plants now potted.

Candle: The elongate new-growth shoot of pines in mid-spring, containing in compact form the season's growth.

Central leader: The tallest, most vigorous and upright apical shoot of a tree.

Compacted soil: See page 14.

Compost: Decomposed organic material.

Container-grown: A plant that has been grown at least a year in a pot.

Cultivar: A contraction of *cultivated variety.*

Cv., Cvs.: Abbreviated singular and plural of *cultivar.*

Deciduous: For our purposes, a plant that drops its leaves each autumn preparing for dormancy.

Dormancy: The winter (or dry-season) rest period characterized by no vegetative growth.

Dormant oil spray: A product derived from paraffins and sprayed on infested plants to control scale insects, insect eggs, and mites by smothering them. Usually applied while the plant is dormant or just breaking dormancy.

Evergreen: A plant, needle leafed or broad leafed, that keeps its leaves for at least a year.

Exposure: Windy, sunny locations.

Facer plants: A uniform mass or row of low plants used to block the view of an unsightly base. They are selected for uniformity, like hedgeplants, and when used to hide the "legs" of a hedge, they will ideally be a cultivar of the same species as the hedge, with similar foliage.

Fastigiate: A plant exhibiting narrow, upright growth.

Fertilizer: A product containing nitrogen, phosphorus, and potassium, either organic or synthesized, sometimes also containing other essential elements. The three numbers corresponding to nitrogen, phosphorus, and potassium, respectively, such as 5-10-5, refer to the relative percents of those elements.

Finger: See *Candle.*

Fire blight: A bacterial disease especially destructive to members of the Rose family (cotoneaster, hawthorns, flowering quince), characterized by mushy, wet, blackened new growth and rapid dieback of leaves and shoots.

Frost pocket: A low spot in a local landscape into which cold air drains and settles from the surrounding higher land.

Green manure: A fast-growing crop such as clover or rye that is plowed under (or dug under) before it matures, to improve the soil in preparation for planting.

Harden-off: The process by which a current season's growth prepares to survive stress such as winter or a dry season.

Healing-in: The practice of crowding newly dug or purchased plants in a sheltered place and covering their roots or containers with soil or mulch when planting will be delayed for more than a few days.

Hedgeplant: Any plant capable of being used in a hedge.

Low-maintenance: Describes a hedge of relatively slow, dense growth. See pages 16-17.

Massing: Refers to planting several or many plants of one type together in a landscape, usually "filler" plants with one- or two-season interest.

Mulch: A substance placed around plants on the soil surface to prevent weed growth, slow water loss, and improve the appearance.

Naturalize: Refers to the process by which landscape plants spread from their original planting and establish themselves in new areas.

Palmate: Here, leaflets arising from a single point, like the fingers of a hand.

Peat humus: The next stage of decomposition after peat moss — a poor mulch but an excellent soil additive. It is crumbly and non-fibrous, unlike peat moss.

Peat moss: Sphagnum and other peat bog mosses in partially decomposed form — some original plant structures are still recognizable. An excellent soil additive.

pH: See pages 14-15.

Pinnate: Here, leaflets arising at alternate or opposite points along a rachis, or leaflet stalk.

Pruning: See pages 23-24, 31-33.

Renewal-pruning: See page 32.

Salt damage: 1. The effect of splashed or blown roadsalt or seaspray near an ocean on the above-ground parts of a plant; symptoms include dieback of the youngest twigs and possible formation of witches' brooms (see) on deciduous plants, and a "burned" appearance and shoot dieback on evergreen plants. 2. Poisoning by salt carried by water in the soil. Symptoms of plants dying of salt poisoning appear slowly; it may be years before the plants show the stunted, thoroughly sick look of salt poisoning. Early signs include a bluish cast to the leaves and browning of leaf edges.

Scale: A sucking-insect group with species that attack most types of plants. Natural insect predators usually keep them under control, but occasionally they get out of hand and must be sprayed with a dormant oil.

Shearing: Pruning done by electric shears.

Single-purpose hedge: A loose term implying a hedge with only one feature other than being a barrier, such as flowers, fall color, etc.

Soil conditions: Refers to moisture levels, drainage.

Soil type: See pages 15-16.

Sour: Here, refers to acidic soil.

Specimen plant: A choice shrub or tree used as a focal point in a landscape. It will usually be a plant with four-season interest.

Spider mites: Tiny, often microscopic, sucking arachnids that cause the most trouble in hot, dry weather. Symptoms include spotting or yellowing of the foliage. Usually hosing with a hard spray is enough to reduce the population; various insecticides also work.

Spp.: Plural abbreviation of *species.*

Sucker: A fast-growing, upright shoot from a root or the base of the trunk or main stem.

Sweet: Here, refers to basic soil. Ground limestone is called a *sweetening agent* because it makes acidic soil more basic, or alkaline.

Terminal growth: The part of a branch or stem farthest from the roots.

Top dressing: Fertilizer or mulch applied to the soil surface.

Urban conditions: Includes polluted, soil-compacted, warmer, and drier conditions.

Variety: A variant within a species.

Well-drained: Soil through which water percolates easily.

Wet soil: Soil with standing water part of the year.

Witches' brooms: Abnormal plant growths that look like brooms; they can be caused by salt damage.

Zone: See pages 11-12.

BIBLIOGRAPHY

Anderson, Susan Eldridge. *An Approach to the Design of Urban Open Spaces...* University of Massachusetts: Amherst, 1974.

Aul, Henry B. *How to Plan Modern Home Grounds.* New York: Sheridan House, 1959.

Brett, William Samuel. *Small City Gardens.* London: Abeland-Schuman, 1967.

Conover, Herbert S. *The Grounds Maintenance Handbook* (3rd ed.). New York: McGraw-Hill, 1977.

Denison, Ervin Loren. *Principles of Horticulture.* New York: Macmillan, 1958.

Dirr, Michael A. *Manual of Woody Landscape Plants.* Champaign, Ill.: Stipes Publishing Co., 1977.

Dirr, Michael A. *Photographic Manual of Woody Landscape Plants.* Champaign, Ill.: Stipes Publishing Co., 1978.

Ebersole, Fred, and Virginia Morrell. *Hollies: Versatile Beauty for the Intimate Landscape.* Baltimore: The Holly Society of America, 1974.

Everett, Thomas H. *Encyclopedia of Horticulture.* 10 vols. New York: Garland Publishing Co., 1980.

Favretti, Rudy J., and Joy Putnam Favretti. *Landscapes and Gardens for Historic Buildings.* Nashville: American Association for State and Local History, 1978.

Flint, Harrison L. *Landscape Plants for Eastern North America.* New York: John Wiley & Sons, 1983.

Gaut, Alfred. *Seaside Planting of Trees and Shrubs.* New York: Charles Scribner's Sons, 1907.

Gorer, Richard. *Trees and Shrubs.* London: David and Charles, 1976.

Hasselkus, E. R. "Hedge Cotoneaster," *Urban Horticulture News,* University of Wisconsin Extension, 35 (1979).

Hasselkus, E. R. "Salt Injury to Landscape Plants," University of Wisconsin Extension Pamphlet A2970.

Hillier, Harold G. *Hillier's Manual of Trees and Shrubs* (5th ed.). New York: Van Nostrand Reinhold, 1981.

Janick, Jules. *Horticultural Science* (2nd ed.). San Francisco: W. H. Freeman, 1972.

Jensen, Jens. *Siftings*. Chicago: R. F. Seymour, 1939.

Kammerer, E. L. "Twelve Superior Clipped Hedges," *Bulletin of Popular Information*, Morton Arboretum, 7 (1957).

Liberty Hyde Bailey Hortorium. *Hortus Third*. New York: Macmillan, 1976.

Lloyd, Nathaniel. *Garden Craftmanship in Yew and Box*. London: Ernest Renn, 1925.

Loudon, John Claudius. *An Encyclopedia of Gardening*. London, 1927.

Low-Maintenance Gardening. Ed. by Sunset Books, Menlo Park, Calif., 1974.

Masengarb, John Vogt. "Formal Hedges for Northern Illinois," *Plant Information Bulletin*, Morton Arboretum (1980).

Nicol, Walter. *The Practical Planter*. Edinburgh, 1799.

Phillips, C. E. Lucas, and Peter Barber. *Ornamental Shrubs*. New York: Van Nostrand Reinhold, 1981.

Pirone, Pascal P. *Diseases and Pests of Ornamental Plants* (5th ed.). New York: John Wiley & Sons, 1978.

Robinette, Gary O. *Evergreen Form Studies*. New York: Van Nostrand Reinhold, 1983.

Scott, Donald H. *Air Pollution Injury to Plant Life*. Washington, D.C.: National Landscape Association, 1973.

Spangler, Ronald L., and Jerry Riperda. *Landscape Plants for Central and Northeastern U.S., Including Lower and Eastern Canada*. Minneapolis: Burgess Publishing Co., 1977.

Viertel, Arthur T. *Trees, Shrubs and Vines*. Syracuse: Syracuse University Press, 1970.

Wilson, Helen Van Pelt. *Color for Your Winter Yard and Garden*. New York: Charles Scribner's Sons, 1978.

Wyman, Donald. "The Best Plants for Hedges," *American Nurseryman*, 121(1) 9, 1969.

Wyman, Donald. *Wyman's Gardening Encyclopedia*. New York: Macmillan, 1977.

INDEX

Page numbers in italics indicate illustrations or tables.
Page numbers in bold indicate primary descriptions of plants.